Radical Humanism and Generous Tolerance

Soyinka on Religion and Human Solidarity

Celucien L. Joseph

Hamilton Books

An Imprint of
Rowman & Littlefield
Lanham • Boulder • New York • Toronto • Plymouth, UK

Copyright © 2017 by Hamilton Books
4501 Forbes Boulevard, Suite 200, Lanham, Maryland 20706
Hamilton Books Acquisitions Department (301) 459-3366

Unit A, Whitacre Mews, 26-34 Stannary Street,
London SE11 4AB, United Kingdom

All rights reserved
Printed in the United States of America
British Library Cataloguing in Publication Information Available

Library of Congress Control Number: 2016953263
ISBN: 978-0-7618-6858-3 (pbk : alk. paper)—ISBN: 978-0-7618-6859-0 (electronic)

Excerpt(s) from ART, DIALOGUE, AND OUTRAGE: ESSAYS ON LITERATURE AND CULTURE by Wole Soyinka, copyright © 1988, 1993 by Wole Soyinka.. Used by permission of Pantheon Books, an imprint of the Knopf Doubleday Publishing Group, a division of Penguin Random House LLC. All rights reserved.

∞™ The paper used in this publication meets the minimum requirements of American National Standard for Information Sciences Permanence of Paper for Printed Library Materials, ANSI/NISO Z39.48-1992.

To my two daughters: Abigail Sarah-Gabriella and Emily Danielle,
and my two sons: Terrence Matthew and Joshua Sebastien.
May you grow to become agents of peace and transformation!

Contents

Acknowledgments — vii

Introduction: Rethinking Wole Soyinka and His Engagement with Religion — 1

1 "Shipwreck of Faith": The Religious Vision and Ideas of Wole Soyinka — 13

2 Against Violence: The Arrogance of Faith and Religious Imperialism — 39

3 Soyinka's Interpretation of Ancestral Faith: Values and Meaning in African Traditional Religions — 53

4 In Praise of Shalom and Human Solidarity: The Logic of Radical Humanism, and The Value of Generous Tolerance — 71

Appendix: Wole Soyinka: Chronology — 87

Bibliography — 97

Index — 101

About the Author — 103

Acknowledgments

Last year in 2015, the general editor, Itibari M. Zulu of *The Journal of Pan African Studies* (now known as *Africology: The Journal of Pan African Studies*) (*AJPAS*) had invited me to serve as the guest editor for a special issue on Wole Soyinka to celebrate his eightieth birthday. The published issue was entitled "Rethinking Wole Soyinka: 81 Years of Protracted Engagement" (Volume 8, Number 5, September 2015). It was a great pleasure to collaborate with a group of fine scholars from different parts of the world to think critical about the significance of and contributions of Soyinka to the field of knowledge and learning. These thinkers have contributed seven excellent chapters to celebrate the achievements, works, and legacy of this eminent African writer, thinker, critic, humanist, human rights advocate, Nobel prize recipient, and man of letter. I have learned a lot from their contributions, which provided better clarity, precision, and understanding about the importance of Soyinka's work.

Continuing with Soyinka's legacy, *Radical Humanism and Generous Tolerance: Soyinka on Religion and Human Solidarity* explores the religious dimensions of Wole Soyinka. It investigates his engagements with the Humanist tradition, African traditional religions, and in particular, his discourse on religious violence and extremism. However, the book accentuates Soyinka's manifold contributions to cultivate planetary peace and love, and human solidarity, what I have phrased "radical humanism and generous tolerance." Few writers have written about the religious vision and ideas of Soyinka in his non-fiction writings. It is the goal of this little book to fill this intellectual gap and affirm a pivotal aspect of Soyinka's thinking.

I would like to thank many friends who have provided constructive feedback and intellectual insights in the production of this book. I'm appreciative to the editor of *AJPAS* who has given the permission to republish my essay in this volume.[1] My wife Katia of 13 years and my children (Terrence, Joshua, Abigail, and Emily) have been supportive of my work as a writer, scholar, and researcher. Most importantly, I'm a husband and father. I'm thankful for their patience, understanding, grace, and love toward me. May God continue strengthening our family and mutual love!

NOTE

1. It is entitled "The Arrogance of Faith and Religious Imperialism: Soyinka's Radical Theistic Humanism and Generous Tolerance," *JPAS*, Volume 8, Number 5 (September, 2015): 19–63.

Introduction

Rethinking Wole Soyinka and His Engagement with Religion

For many thinkers, the twenty-first century is best characterized as a world of religious terror and the fear of religious fanaticism. Religious violence and extremism is a rampant phenomenon in the modern world. We who live in the West or in progressive and secular societies are not exempt from this global epidemic. Religious violence has deepened human suffering and pain, and hindered frank ecumenical dialogue and peace talk among the nations and people of different faiths or religious commitment. On one hand, it is true that religious violence is global, cross-cultural, transnational, and interreligious. On the other hand, we continue to ask each other this question: what must we do collaboratively to put an end to the problem of religious violence in the world today?

Nonetheless, we do not lose hope nor have we stopped striving to create better human solidarity and collaboration desperately needed today in the world. We continue to inquire about a solution or possible solutions or the solution to the conundrum of religious extremism and terror in the world. Will there be an end to religious violence and the fear of religious fanaticism? Is it possible to live without religious violence? We are certain about what we want and that which will contribute to human flourishing and global shalom. We want peace! We and our children want to live in a world absent of (or the fear of) violence, terror, hatred, animosity, and social sins. We want to live in a society that is not menaced by religious fanatics or extremists. The aim of this book is to engage these various critical and interrelated issues, with an emphasis on the religious vision and ideas of Soyinka. In *Radical Humanism and Generous Tolerance*, we seek for wisdom and enduring human values in the writings of Soyinka and learn from him about the nature and dynamics religion, and religious tolerance. The writings of Soyinka are particularly relevant today in the cultivation of cross-cultural dialogue and transnational human solidarity, and the promotion of interreligious peace and understanding between people of different faiths. The book highlights Soyinka's argument to embrace humanism as an alternative to religious exclusivism and absolute claims, and his clarion call for generous tolerance, and religious inclusivism.

Akinwande Oluwole Babatunde Soyinka's ("Wole Soyinka") is a Nigerian writer, playwright, poet, human rights activist, cultural critic, and public intellectual who was awarded the Nobel Prize in Literature in 1986, becoming the first person in Africa to receive the award.[1] An activist in Nigeria's fight for independence, Soyinka was imprisoned in solitary confinement from 1967 to 1969 for writing an article that called for a cease-fire. To this day he is involved in the politics of Nigeria. As a prolific writer and a man of extraordinary talents and skills, Soyinka has published and produced plays, poetry collections, essays, novels, memoirs, short stories, and film projects; academic and historical books. He has three honorary doctorates (University of Leeds, Harvard, and Princeton); taught at universities in Africa, the United Kingdom, the United States, and he is presently Professor in Residence at Loyola Marymount University in Los Angeles, California.

Born in July 13, 1934 in Abeokuta, Nigeria, Soyinka was raised in a religious environment in Abeokuta, Nigeria to Christian parents: Samuel Ayodele (father) and Grace Eniola Soyinka (mother). Soyinka in his important work Of Africa describes the religious tolerance and interfaith understanding between Nigerian Christians and Muslims existed in his hometown: "My Christian family lived just next door to Muslims. We celebrated Ramadan with Muslims; they celebrated Christmas with Christians. This is how I grew up."[2] As a child in Ake, and all the way through secondary school and beyond, he remembers having witnessed and enjoyed "the harmonious cohabitation of diverse religious beliefs, the reign of religious zealotry, enveloping and consuming entire communities, has become a way of life."[3] While Soyinka's milieu was very religious and culturally accommodative, he was inquisitive about the meaning of religion, and its role in both political and civil society.

Soyinka's father was the Headmaster of a local school in Ake and a devoted religious man. His mother, whom he affectionately called "Wild Christian," in his second autobiography Ake: The Years of Childhood, because of her religious piety and unrelenting commitment to Christianity, "came from one of the most distinguished Anglican families in western Nigeria; his maternal grandfather was a minister in the local Anglican church."[4] Anglicanism penetrated the African soil in Nigeria by coercion when British colonizers used the instrumentalization of religion for political purposes and to subjugate the Africans, resulting in the alteration of African traditional life, cultures, and religious practices. Originated from British colonial rule at the beginning in the nineteenth century, the modern state of Nigeria became formally postcolonial and independent in 1960. Unfortunately, Nigeria would plunge into a devastated civil war that lasted for three years (967–1970).

For his secondary education, Soyinka attended the local Abeokuta Grammar School, from 1944 to 1954. He studied Literature and languages (French and Greek) at University College in Ibadan, from 1952 to 1954. After fulfilling his preparatory university studies at Government College in Ibadan in 1954, Soyinka moved to England to pursue academic studies in drama and English literature at the University of Leeds. He worked in British theatre while living away from his native land, serving as a dramaturgist at the Royal Court Theater in London (1958–1959).

Soyinka graduated with a B.A. in English Honors in 1957. Granted "a Rockefeller fellowship on New Year's Day of 1960 to research traditional dramatic forms,"[5] Soyinka returned to Nigeria the same year. Soyinka has written some of the most politically-and socially-engaged plays in the history of African drama. While the Nigerian playwright and actor Oloye Hubert Adedeji Ogunde (1916–1990) is traditionally called the "Father of Nigerian the father of Nigerian theatre, or the father of contemporary Yoruba theatre,"[6] Wole Soyinka has labored tiredly to develop it and give it an international space. Through the art of performance theatre, and the writing of acclaimed plays such as Death and the King's Horseman, and A Dance of the Forests, Soyinka engaged African traditional life, cultures, politics, worldviews, politics, and exposed the Continent's religious life. More particularly, Soyinka explored the cosmology and moral vision of the Yoruba people, and the politics of the newly-founded postcolonial state of Nigeria. As he observes in his one of his memoirs You Must Set Forth at Dawn:

> It was good fortune that I could return home—where the gods were still only in a state of hibernation . . . I penetrated east, north, south at will and toured the entire West African coast on the trail of festivals and performing companies, keeping touch with gods and goddesses everywhere and celebrating their seasons . . . Like the many faces of Ogun, god of the road, the road was also a violent host. The road and I thus became partners in the quest for an extended self-discovery. I stared into the many faces of death, but most often death just taking its leave, its back indifferently turned on heartbreak and destruction . . . Ogun had other plans for me, however.[7]

Soyinka is a political writer and public activist. His public and intellectual activism is preoccupied with the political life and future of politics in Nigeria and other countries in Africa. Through his prolific writings and plays, he challenges and denounces totalitarian and authoritarian administrations in

Nigeria, as well as other dictators in the Continent. Upon his return in Nigeria in 1960, he founded the theatre group called "The 1960 Masks," which would serve as a vehicle of protest against oppressive regimes. After serving a one year post as a Lecturer in English at the University of Life, he resigned from the post in protest of the undemocratic public policies of the Western Nigerian regional government. In 1964, Soyinka became very active in Nigerian politics. Serving as a Senior Lecturer at the University of Lagos, in 1965, he was briefly arrested for political protest.

When the Nigerian civil war begins in 1966, Soyinka published a controversial article demanding cease-fire. He was accused of conspiring with the Biafra rebels to overthrown the current administration. Consequently, he was held in prison for 22 months as a political prisoner. In January 15, 1966, the first military coup overthrew the First Republic and established the Ironsi regime. In a little over six months (July 29, 1966), the second military coup established the Gowon regime. Soyinka was released in prison in 1969; he became an expatriate in the neighboring country of Ghana. From 1966 to 1990, the people and country of Nigeria experienced eight military coups which had had a tremendous impact on the life, politics, and economy of the country and its relationships with other countries in the Continent, as well as with the international community. In addition, religious conflict (i.e. March 1987, April 1991, etc.) between Christians and Muslims remains an uncompleted task in the country. Soyinka's life has been shaped by these historic events and administrations. The hopeful Wole Soyinka maintains that "Education remains a critical aspect in the development of any nation as it unlocks the thinking canals of our youth. However, a holistic education that encompasses the ability to help children appreciate their humanity and show empathy to their fellow human beings is what guarantees a prosperous nation."[8]

After a period of almost six years, he returned to Nigeria in 1975. From 1975 to 1994, he was uninterruptedly involved in the cultural, literary, and political life of his country. In 1994, he fled Nigeria to save his life from the current dictator. In 1995, he protested against the cancellation by the military regime of the federal elections won by Moshood Abiola. He launched an international campaign against the Nigerian dictatorship. In March 1997, he was charged with treason and sentenced to death in absentia by the Nigerian military regime of Sani Abacha. Eventually, he returned to Nigeria in 1998. Soyinka systematically documents these incidents and discusses his political activism and transactions, covering the 1960s to the 1990s, in three "political memoirs:" The Man Died: Prison Notes of Wole Soyinka (1972), Ibadan: The Penkelmes Years: A Memoir, 1946–1965 (1994), and You Must Set Forth at Dawn (2006).

Soyinka has written some of the most politically-and socially-engaged plays in the history of African drama. While the Nigerian playwright and actor Oloye Hubert Adedeji Ogunde (1916–1990) is traditionally called the

"Father of Nigerian the father of Nigerian theatre, or the father of contemporary Yoruba theatre,"[9] Wole Soyinka has labored tiredly to develop it and give it an international space. Through the art of performance theatre, and the writing of acclaimed plays such as Death and the King's Horseman, and A Dance of the Forests, Soyinka engaged African traditional life, cultures, politics, worldviews, politics, and exposed the Continent's religious life. More particularly, Soyinka explored the cosmology and moral vision of the Yoruba people, and the politics of the newly-founded postcolonial state of Nigeria. As he observes in one of his memoirs You Must Set Forth at Dawn:

> It was good fortune that I could return home—where the gods were still only in a state of hibernation . . . I penetrated east, north, south at will and toured the entire West African coast on the trail of festivals and performing companies, keeping touch with gods and goddesses everywhere and celebrating their seasons . . . Like the many faces of Ogun, god of the road, the road was also a violent host. The road and I thus became partners in the quest for an extended self-discovery. I stared into the many faces of death, but most often death just taking its leave, its back indifferently turned on heartbreak and destruction . . . Ogun had other plans for me, however.[10]

In five autobiographies, ranging from 1972 to 2007,[11] Soyinka meticulously chronicles his life in Nigeria and beyond its borders, the plight of the African people, and his numerous encounters and interactions with his family, friends, enemies, strangers, and the cultures and peoples of the world. The passion of Soyinka is not the pursuit of personal fame but the quest for and preservation of freedom and human rights on behalf of the African people and the human race. In The Burden of Memory, The Muse of Forgiveness, published in 1999, he penned these heartrending words as he attempts to make sense of memory in the time of conflict, despair, and healing:

> Every landmark is a testament of history, and in our indelible instance—From Goree through the slave forts of Ghana to Zanzibar—every fort and stockade, increasingly turned into museums, is filled with grim evocations of this passage of our history. They are indices of Truth, an essence and a reality that offer any peoples, however impoverished, a value in itself, a value that, especially rooted in anguish and sacrifice, may dictate a revolve for redemption and strategies for social regeneration.[12]

Soyinka urges the Africans, people of African descent in the Diaspora, and friends of humanity not to demean the severity of the wounds and sufferings of the people in continental Africa. He wrote these powerful words in the 1990s in the midst of conflict and antagonism that have transformed the relationships and interplays between the African people and the African countries:

> It is not possible for us to ignore the actuality of brutal conflicts on our own continent—some as blatantly race derived as those between Senegal and Mauritania within this decade, and the even more intractable ongoing conflict in the Sudan, a conflict that has entailed over three decades of carnage, with the possible consequences of social disintegration of an enduring nature. The indigenous culture of Sudan is today imperiled as never before! Does this matter? Have we a duty to be concerned? Or threatened?[13]

In the same line of thought, Soyinka is internationally known as a humanist, a protagonist of human rights, and a champion of human dignity. At the World Humanist Congress held in 2014, Wole Soyinka was honored with the International Humanist Award from The British Humanist Association. In presenting the award to Soyinka, Patricia Rogers, the trustee of the organization, defended the organization's choice in this statement: "In the sharpest possible contrast to the terrorist Boko Haram's dichotomous disavowal of 'western education' as alien to their world, Soyinka has long been the intellectual leader of distinctively African voices within the universal Enlightenment tradition."[14] Soyinka is a fierce critic of religious terrorism and fundamentalism, as well as a promoter of religious tolerance and religious pluralism.

It is good to inform the readers that the message of Soyinka's acceptance speech should be understood within the cultural backdrop and historical violence of the Nigerian Islamist extremist group known as Boko Haram. In April 2014, the religious extremists of Boko Haram abducted 276 schools girls from a learning center in Chibok, Borno. Hence, we can anticipate Soyinka to denounce the crime in his speech. In response to this historic crime, Soyinka makes the following observations:

> We are not yet speaking our own truths to Religion or else, are failing to find a language that penetrates, in an effective way, the hearing of that minority that needs to hear them, those whose mission is to set this palpable world on fire, through adherence to a vaporous hereafter where their incendiary mission in the substantive here and now will be rewarded. Humanism requires a new tactical language, and what that language expresses requires a drastic shift in emphasis. We must take on the duty of telling the enemy openly: it is not spiritual fulfillment that you seek but—Power. Control. Power in its crudest form. Humanism requires to develop a distinct philosophy of transformative aggression. At this moment in the lives of communities across the globe, taking note of the havoc wreaked daily by the doctrine of religious impunity, there is far too much appeasement and toleration in the language we bring to each confrontation. There comes a time when our humanity accepts that there must be an end to an attitude that is best captured in that Yoruba expression: F'itiju k'arun. Literally that means "contracting a disease through politeness." Translated yet again, this time into the fashionable language of social morbidity that mistakes sophistry for sophistication, it reads simply: Political Correctness.[15]

What is then the proposed remedy to the problem of religious violence in the world? Or how now shall we live in a world characterized by despair and uncertainty? What does Soyinka have to about this violent world and disheartening humanity?

Because of its open-mindedness and tolerant nature to accommodate alien faiths and foreign ideologies, Soyinka proposes African indigenous spirituality and African humanism as a liberative presence in the modern world against the arrogance of faith and religious imperialism, and in a world progressively digressing and evolving meaninglessly. In the chapter entitled "Spirituality of a Continent" in Of Africa, Soyinka praises the irenic nature of African traditional religions and spirituality:

> Religions that lay claim to world stature on certificates of ultimate truth and universality should pause and demand of themselves: Why is it that the worship of Orisa has never, in all these centuries, and even on hostile foreign soil, spawned an irredentist strain? The answer lies of course in the fundamental, accommodative intelligence of the Orisa. We need only contrast this with the catechism of submission that is the pillar of faith in other religions, such as Islam or Christianity.[16]

Furthermore, Soyinka calls for ecumenical dialogue and underscores the value of tolerance, which African spirituality promotes, and that which the religions, peoples, and nations of the world desperately need in order to build stronger societies, create a more perfect international relationships among the nations, and to foster a democratic life and radical new humanism in this present time:

> Tolerance is perhaps the most relevant, the most sorely in demand in our global dilemma . . . Tolerance, in its own right, is at the heart of Ifa, a virtue worth cultivating as a foundational principle of humanistic faith—the catechism of the secular deities, a spirit of accommodativeness . . .
>
> Thus, for all seekers after the peace and security of true community, and the space of serenity that enables the quest after truth, pleading for understanding from the Orisa for this transgression of their timeless scorn of proselytizing, we urge yet again the simple path that was travelled from the soil of the Yoruba across the African landmass to contiguous nations, across the hostile oceans to the edge of the world in the Americas—Go to the Orisa, learn from the Orisa, and be wise.[17]

The collective corpus of Wole Soyinka reveals the soul of the African continent, and embodies what the father of Negritude and Senegale theorist and poet Leopold Sedar Senghor called "The sum total of the values of the civilization of the African World." On the other hand, the writings of Soyinka expose the fear, disappointments, shortcomings, and hopes of the African people, the African Diaspora, and the plight of humanity at large. James

Gibbs has observed that "Much of his work is linked to Yoruba culture and Yoruba concepts. Some of the most obvious examples of the use of Yoruba material and the presence of Yoruba influence show his abiding concern with the Yoruba worldview."[18] Simon Gikandi, in his insightful introduction to the 2003 Norton Critical Edition of Soyinka's Death and the King's Horseman, writes informatively:

> Although he is proud of his African heritage and has been one of the staunchest defenders of African cultural interests, Soyinka has resisted identification with one singular tradition; in both their content and form, his works reflect the multiplicity of sources and references that are very much part of his background and education. In spite of this, Soyinka's works are solidly located in the cosmic systems of the Yoruba people of western Nigeria and the Republic of Benin. Of all modern African writers, Soyinka is the one whose works derive their power from the essential forces of an African culture; it is impossible to conceive of his work outside Yoruba religious beliefs and systems of thought. At the same time, however, Soyinka is the most cosmopolitan and avant-garde of African playwrights.[19]

The collective work of Wole Soyinka should be interpreted as a poignant and impassioned commentary on the human condition, from the time he published his first short story, "Keffi's Birthday Treat," in 1957 to his continuous engagement in the craft and art of writing.[20] In his insightful text, Climate of Fear: The Quest for Dignity in a Dehumanized World, Soyinka expresses his longing and passion for freedom, democracy, and generous tolerance among the peoples of the world. He envisions a new world, new cultures and societies, and new human narratives in which the peoples and nations of the world could flourish and express their self-agency and determination:

> We consider also a dispensation that enables all humanity to breathe freely, to associate freely, to think freely, and to believe or not to believe without a threat to their existence and without discrimination in their social rights. Implicit in that freedom of association is, difficult as it may be to accept, the right of collective dissociation.[21]

In his quest for human dignity and incisive commentary on the so-called "The Middle East conflict," the Israelite-Palestine conundrum, he penned these provocative words as an urgent call to the international community and both countries to become protagonist of peace and agents of transformation:

> It is becoming impossible to recall a time when death visited this field of incompatibilities in single digits. Let us bear that in mind as we recall the response of Israel's main backer, the United States, to the escalation of this belligerence, so rooted in disdain that it literally bared an opponent, a belea-

guered leader of his people, of all the rags of authority—reverting to our language of conflict bargaining—and left him not a stitch to cover his nudity. Madeleine Albright, then secretary of state, read a statement on behalf of the U.S. government that failed to recall the deaths of Palestinians, failed to share with the world any thought of regret for their death, even as she mourned and commiserated with the Israeli government on the death of two of its soldiers. Such unstatesmanlike and insensitivity, such a crass lacuna in the history of global relationships, which was justly and bitterly seized upon by the secretary-general of the Arab League, reinforced the glaring question on the chains of the United States to be an evenhanded partner for peace with the rest of the world.[22]

For Soyinka, the historic antagonism between the two countries can be explained in terms of lack of respect for human dignity and human life. As he explains with clarity and precision:

Dignity is simply another face of freedom, and thus the observe of power and domination, that axis of human relationship that is equally sustained by fear—its poles doomed to remain in permanent conflict, yet complement each other . . . I offered a contrast in the feeling of helplessness that one obtains when Nature itself is the force of domination, as opposed to when any human, an equal of others in most ways, takes on the role of dominator or dispenser of life and death, and robs one of the faculty of volition. We need such reminders from time to time to ward off the supercilious cant of those—mostly the purveyors of terror, state or quasi-state, and the vicarious undertakers of human wastage—who wave off human trauma with some profound logic that is presumably embedded in comments such as "After all, one sudden earthquake or flood kills more people than even a year long civil conflict in Liberia or Chechnya." Neither death nor suffering is at issue.[23]

Radical Humanism and Generous Tolerance presents Soyinka as a religious critic and transnational public international whose main concerns entail the promotion of public peace, mutual tolerance, and human dignity through a careful examination of his religious writings. It investigates Soyinka's response to religious violence, terror, and imperialism in his non-fiction writings. The book advances the argument that in response to religious imperialism and absolutism in the world, Soyinka relies heavily on the wisdom and principles of two worldviews and ideologies: African indigenous humanism and African traditional religion and spirituality. It also suggests that the theoretical notions of radical theistic humanism and generous tolerance best summarize Soyinka's ideals and systems of thought on this matter. Unlike Western humanism that is antisupernaturalistic, African humanism is informed by religious metaphysics—the religious value and life of the African people. Soyinka's humanism is trapped within the religious ethos and sensibility and moral vision of the Yoruba people.

Chapter one analyzes the religious environment of Soyinka, and his curiosity for things religious, and ultimately, his renouncement of the Christian faith and the God of his parents. It also chronicles the progression of Soyinka's faith, and his critical reflections on the nature and dynamics of religion. Soyinka reclaims his African traditional religions and spirituality, contrary to the imported religion of Islam and Christianity in the African continent. Chapter two studies Soyinka's critique of religion in general, and of religious violence and extremism in particular. It also examines his argument for humanism and religious inclusivism as a response to religious terror and religious exclusivism. Chapter three is an exploration of Soyinka's dialogue with African traditional religions and spirituality. This chapter is a continuity of chapter one: Soyinka's "return to ancestral faith." This chapter establishes the values of African traditional religions and spirituality in the non-fictive works of Soyinka—as the subject relates to peace and harmony in the world. Soyinka argues that African traditional religions could be used as a catalyst to promote interreligious compromise and solidarity, and that they contribute to the preservation of human life and the promotion of global peace. Chapter four is an elaboration of what's already been discussed in the previous chapter, chiefly Soyinka's radical humanism and generous tolerance. In this chapter, we also explore other facets of these twin ideas in Soyinka's writings. Soyinka brings in conversation the Western Humanist tradition and African indigenous Humanist tradition for the sake of the world, for the sake of global shalom, and for the sake of human flourishing.

Finally, two appendices are included in this volume. Appendix A lists the most important works by Soyinka. The list is structured in chronological order and according to the genre of the work. Next, we offer a general sketch of the most important and historical events in Wole Soyinka's life and career, from the time of his birth in 1934 to his eightieth birthday. Appendix B reproduces Soyinka's speech Wole Soyinka's International Humanist Award acceptance speech, delivered in 2014.

NOTES

1. For important studies on Soyinka, see, Ivor Agyzman-duah, and Ogochukwu Promise (eds), *Essays in Honour of Wole Soyinka at 80* (2014); Biodun Jeyifo (ed), *Perspectives on Wole Soyinka: Freedo m and Complexity* (2006); Onookme Okome (ed), *Ogun's Children: The Literature and Politics of Wole Soyinka Since the Nobel* (2003); Biodun Jeyifo, *Wole Soyinka: Politics, Poetics, and Postcolonialism* (2009); Biodun Jefio, *Conversations with Wole Soyinka* (2001); James Gibbs (ed), *Critical Perspective on Wole Soyinka* (1980); Mpalive-Hangson Msiska, Wole Soyinka (2010).

2. "Wole Soyinka: 'If religion was taken away I'd be happy.'" The Telegraph. 12 Oct 2012. Accessed July 6, 2012. http://www.telegraph.co.uk/culture/hay-festival/9600954/Wole-Soyinka-If-religion-was-taken-away-Id-be-happy.html . Wole Soyinka was the invited speaker to the Hay Festival in Mexico, which occurred in October 2012.

3. Soyinka, *Of Africa*, 185.

4. Gikandi, "Introduction," in Soyinka, *Death and the King's Horseman*, xi.
5. Soyinka, *You Must Set Forth at Dawn*, 46.
6. Banham and Hill (eds), *The Cambridge Guide to African and Caribbean Theatre*, 76.
7. Soyinka, *You Must Set Forth at Dawn: A Memoir*, 46, 49, 112.
8. "Access Bank hosts Professor Wole Soyinka in Ghana." *Ghana Business News*. 3 July 2015.https://www.ghanabusinessnews.com/2015/07/03/access-bank-hosts-professor-wole-soyinka-in-ghana/
9. Banham and Hill (eds), *The Cambridge Guide to African and Caribbean Theatre*, 76.
10. Soyinka, *You Must Set Forth at Dawn: A Memoir*, 46, 49, 112.
11. Soyinka's five autobiographies include the following: *The Man Died: Prison Notes of Wole Soyinka* (1972), *Ake: The Years of Childhood* (1981), *Isara: A Voyage Around "Essay"* (1989), *Ibadan: The Penkelmes Years: A Memoir, 1946–1965* (1994), and *You Must Set Forth at Dawn* (2006).
12. Soyinka, *The Burden of Memory, The Muse of Forgiveness*, 59–60.
13. Ibid., 61.
14. Interested readers can read the entire speech online: http://iheu.org/wole-soyinkas-international-humanist-award-acceptance-speech-full-text/
15. The International Humanist and Ethical Union (IHEU). 12 August, 2014. Interested readers can read the entire speech online: http://iheu.org/wole-soyinkas-international-humanist-award-acceptance-speech-full-text/
16. Soyinka, *Of Africa*, 164–5.
17. Ibid., 165, 168.
18. Gibbs, "Introduction," in James Gibbs, *Critical Perspectives on Wole Soyinka*, 3.
19. Ibid., viii.
20. For a brief chronology of the most important events in Soyinka's life, see "Brief Chronology of Wole Soyinka, 1935–Present." To learn more about his writings and play productions, see Appendix A: "Wole Soyinka: Chronology and Selected Bibliography."
21. Soyinka, *The Open Sore of a Continent*, 142.
22. Soyinka, *Climate of Fear*, 103.
23. Ibid., 105.

Chapter One

"Shipwreck of Faith"

The Religious Vision and Ideas of Wole Soyinka

The objective of chapter one is to investigate the religious vision and ideas of Wole Soyinka in selected non-fiction writings. While African spirituality is deployed as a literary trope in Soyinka's creative works and dramatic masterpieces such as *Death and the King's Horseman, and A Dance of the Forests*, scholars have given scarce attention to his engagement with religion in his non-fiction productions. Consequently, there exists both an intellectual and literary gap to bridge Soyinka's religious ideas expressed in his fictions and those articulated in his various memoirs and essays. This chapter as the remaining part of the book is an attempt to fill the void.

First, the chapter proposes the notions of radical skepticism and religious inclusivism as symbolic markers to describe Soyinka's perspective on religion and his shipwreck of faith. His witness of religious violence and fanaticism in his home country of Nigeria and the host countries outside of his native land had shaped his religious experience and altered his religious vision. To call Wole Soyinka a radical agnostic and religious inclusivist in the humanist tradition is to confront the uneasiness and ambivalence of religion that had marked both his adolescent and adult life. Secondly, the chapter argues that Soyinka's abandonment of his Anglican faith, the "imported religion" of his childhood and Nigerian parents, was a consequence of his reevaluation of the merits and liberalism of his ancestral faith: the Yoruba religious tradition and spirituality. Thirdly, the chapter contends that Soyinka rejected the Christian faith because of a theological crisis he encountered both as a teenager in Ake (his hometown), and as a student at the University College in Ibadan.

As it is the purpose of this book, this present chapter resituates Soyinka's religious sensibility not in the tradition of the Abrahamic religions but within the religious worldview and cultural framework of African indigenous faiths and spirituality. Finally, both the book and this chapter in particular present Wole Soyinka as a religious critic, public intellectual and radical theistic humanist who called for the eradication of all religions in modern society.

SOYINKA'S FAITH AND SHIPWRECK OF FAITH

Akinwande Oluwole Babatunde Soyinka ("Wole Soyinka") was raised in a religious environment in Abeokuta, Nigeria. Soyinka's parents, Samuel Ayodele (father) and Grace Eniola Soyinka (mother) were Christians who embraced Anglicanism as a religious affiliation. Anglicanism is a religious denomination within Western Protestant Christianity; it is affiliated with the Church of England. It emerged in the 16th century during the English religious Reformation as a result of a split over religious issues during the reins of three British monarchs: Henry VIII, Edward VI, and Mary I. In particular, Anglicanism declared its autonomy from the Holy See during the historic religious treaty in the reign of Elizabeth I.

Anglicanism penetrated the African soil in Nigeria by coercion when British Christian slavers and colonizers used the instrumentalization of religion for political purposes and to subjugate the Africans, resulting in the alteration of African traditional religions and practices, and social fabric. The modern state of Nigeria became formally postcolonial and independent in 1960. Wole Soyinka was born in July 13, 1934, and was nurtured in the teachings of colonial British-Nigerian Christianity. Yet, one could resolutely conclude that he is a legitimate child of both eras: the colonial and postcolonial Nigerian Christianity.

In *Isara: A Voyage Around "Essay,"* his second autobiography, Soyinka recounts various moments of religious interaction and experience of his life including regular attendance of Sunday school, religious revivals, and local religious services. Soyinka attended a Christian school for his secondary education, the local Abeokuta Grammar School, from 1944 to 1954. In his scholastic pursuit, he was trained in the principles of Christian theology, morality, and worldview. In an important essay, he explains that as a youth, he regularly attended fundamentalist Christian sect churches in Nigeria known as the "Cherubim and Seraphim."[1] For his play *Brother Jero*, he contacted several of these churches, and reported that "I often attended the services or watched their ecstatic dancing through windows."[2]

Soyinka also mentions that some form of religious tolerance and interfaith understanding between Nigerian Christians and Muslims existed in his hometown: "My Christian family lived just next door to Muslims. We celebrated Ramadan with Muslims; they celebrated Christmas with Christians. This is how I grew up."[3] As a child in Ake, and all the way through secondary school and beyond, he remembers having witnessed and enjoyed "the harmonious cohabitation of diverse religious beliefs, the reign of religious zealotry, enveloping and consuming entire communities, has become a way of life."[4] Soyinka's environment was very religious and accommodative; yet, he was inquisitive about the faith that had nurtured him in his upbringing.

As a Yoruba, Soyinka grew up in the syncretic religious culture of Nigeria and was very much embroiled in African cosmology and values. As he asserts in an interview in 2002 with the South African journalist Peter Godwin: "I gravitated towards what I saw was a cohesive system of a certain relationship of human beings to environment, a respect for humanity in general."[5] In the process of assessing the religious lessons imparted from childhood,[6] he adopted Ogun as "his companion deity,"[7] and worked at Ife in Yorubaland, "a spiritual center of the Yoruba, [which] is conveniently symbolic."[8] In his fourth autobiography, *You Must Set Forth at Dawn*, with literary beauty and dazzling rhetoric, he concedes that the metallurgy and lyric arts god of the Yoruba pantheon is his divine partner in crime:

> The Suggestions that I was possessed quite early in life by the creative-combative deity Ogun is a familiar commentary some literary critics who stretch my creative fascination with that deity, undeniable in my works, beyond its literary purlieu . . . My adopted muse would remain Ogun, but only he of the biting lyric. Alas, that willful deity would refuse to bow to moral preferences within his dual nature![9]

In the introductory paragraph of the first chapter of *Myth, Literature, and the African World*, he praises the African gods for facilitating literary inspiration and creativity:

> I shall begin by commemorating the gods for their self-sacrifice on the altar of literature, and in so doing press them into further service on behalf of human society, and its quest for the explication of being . . . They control the aesthetic considerations of ritual enactment and give to every performance a multi-level experience of the mystical and the mundane.[10]

James Gibbs comes to the conclusion that "Much of his work is linked to Yoruba culture and Yoruba concepts. Some of the most obvious examples of the use of Yoruba material and the presence of Yoruba influence show his abiding concern with the Yoruba worldview."[11] Simon Gikandi, in his insightful introduction to the 2003 Norton Critical Edition of Soyinka's *Death and the King's Horseman*, writes informatively:

> Although he is proud of his African heritage and has been one of the staunchest defenders of African cultural interests, Soyinka has resisted identification

with one singular tradition; in both their content and form, his works reflect the multiplicity of sources and references that are very much part of his background and education. In spite of this, Soyinka's works are solidly located in the cosmic systems of the Yoruba people of western Nigeria and the Republic of Benin. Of all modern African writers, Soyinka is the one whose works derive their power from the essential forces of an African culture; it is impossible to conceive of his work outside Yoruba religious beliefs and systems of thought. At the same time, however, Soyinka is the most cosmopolitan and avant-garde of African playwrights.[12]

To complement his commentary on the religious environment which had shaped Soyinka's religious ideas and sensibilities, we need to turn to another passage by Gikandi in which he underscores the prominence of African spirituality in Soyinka's literary corpus:

> Christianity and its belief systems may not be a marked feature of Soyinka's drama except perhaps as a subject of satire in his comical plays or the source of aberration and alienation in his metaphysical plays, but it was a central element in his early life and education. It is not an exaggeration to say that Soyinka came from one of the most religious and Westernized families in colonial Nigeria. On the other hand, Soyinka's paternal grandfather led a life that was guided by ancient Yoruba beliefs and practices, and it was through extended visits to this side of his family that Soyinka was exposed to the rituals and cosmologies of his people.[13]

After fulfilling his preparatory university studies at Government College in Ibadan in 1954, Soyinka moved to England to pursue academic studies in drama and English literature at the University of Leeds. Soyinka probably lost his faith as a University student at the University College in Ibadan, and most certainly in London, where he was exposed to a sea of ideas and "texts of reason" in the tradition of Western nontheistic humanism that have challenged his childhood religious experience and belief in the Christian God; as he reports in his autobiography:

> Much as he would have preferred to resume his place in the choir, especially when it rehearsed the great anthems—Haydn's *Creation* exerted a permanent spell on him—he was increasingly repulsed by the ultimate end of most recitals, and he gradually withdrew.
> It was in the very process of writing the article that ended his doubts, and it branded him for ever in the eyes of not a few, as the much heralded and dreaded anti-christ. He titled it: Ideals of an Atheist and, to make matters worse, it won the essay prize. For once, it was not an achievement that he could even dream of advertising at home.[14]

As previously noted, his inclination toward the nonreligious was evident. After three years of study at Ibadan, Soyinka graduated with a B.A. in English Honors in 1957. Granted "a Rockefeller fellowship on New Year's Day of 1960 to research traditional dramatic forms,"[15] Soyinka returned to his native land in the same year. Through the art and craft of theatric performances, and the writing of acclaimed plays such as *Death and the King's Horseman*, and *A Dance of the Forests*, Soyinka renounced his Christian faith in which he had been raised and the God of his African parents in order to write the most poetically-divine verses and glorious songs of praise and exaltation to the new divine masters: the Yoruba gods. His allegiance to the Christian God was consequently transferred to other deities. As he ran West toward Africa, he and his theatre team publicly honored the old African deities with the most memorable dramatic lines ever written in the history of African theatre.

> It was good fortune that I could return home—where the gods were still only in a state of hibernation . . . I penetrated east, north, south at will and toured the entire West African coast on the trail of festivals and performing companies, keeping touch with gods and goddesses everywhere and celebrating their seasons . . . Like the many faces of Ogun, god of the road, the road was also a violent host. I stared into the many faces of death, but most often death just taking its leave, its back indifferently turned on heartbreak and destruction . . . Ogun had other plans for me, however.[16]

In a masterpiece article, "Theatre in African Traditional Cultures: Survival Patterns," published in 1982, Soyinka systematically reports various cases of religious terrorism, which he and his travel team encountered in Nigeria. In fact, West African traditional theater was birthed in the labyrinth of religious imperialism and persecution from both Christian and Muslim radicals. For these avatars of religion, West African drama challenged the theology and values of both Christianity and Islam, and "the destructive imperatives of colonialism,"[17] inspired by religion. In the article, he chronicles the hostility of both religions:

> The Muslims, victorious in northern Yorubaland, banned most forms of theatrical performance as contrary to the spirit of Islam. The *Agbejijo, Alarinjo* and allied genres, with their dramatic use of the paraphernalia of carved masks and other representations of ancestral spirits, came most readily under religious disapproval . . . The Christian missionaries had also begun their northward drive, usually only a few steps ahead of the colonial forces. The philistine task begun by the Moslems was rounded out by the Christians' ban on the activities of suspect cults. The Christians went further. They did not content themselves with banning just the dramatic performance; they placed their veto also on indigenous musical instruments—*bata, gangan, dundun* and so on—the very backbone of traditional theatre.[18]

Evidently, Wole Soyinka's religious belief has evolved and tragically altered as he reconsidered the values and merits of African indigenous religions and spirituality, and experienced the reality of African gods in the practical matters of life. Having been exposed to the inevitable external influences and forces—political, intellectual, and religious—, he became cynical about the adopted religion of his youth. As he reports to Godwin, "I gravitated towards a deeper knowledge of the *orisha*, which represents the Yoruba pantheon, very similar ways to the Greek pantheon. You have reprobate deities, beneficent deities. I found that more honest than a kind of unicellular deity of either Christianity or Islam." Soyinka reevaluated the trustworthiness of the God of his parents, and the faithfulness of Deity of the Abrahamic (monotheistic) faiths, as he avowed the African Gods were much more reliable, practical, and manageable. Soyinka turned his back from Christianity because of a theological (God) crisis.

THE PROBLEM OF RELIGIOUS BELIEF AND RELIGIOUS ZEALOTRY

Soyinka's "shipwreck of faith" should not be equated with the idea of religious unbelief or the total rejection of theism as a plausible worldview. This particular mindset toward religion does not embrace Sam Harris's notion that "religious belief may be nothing more than ordinary belief applied to religious content; such beliefs are clearly special in so far as they are deemed special by their adherents."[19] In the words of Daniel Dennett's provocative statement, "Religious belief isn't always belief."[20] Perhaps, we should understand Soyinka's new perspective on religion not so much as a direct attack on religious piety, but it is certainly a challenge to religious fanaticism and zealotry. Soyinka's shipwreck of faith means the complete separation (or renouncement)—both in the psychological and intellectual level—from a despotic and inhumane system that encompasses the religious, cultural, political, economic, and social realm. Such was the nature of colonial Christianity in Nigeria.

Soyinka's crisis of faith and religious cynicism were also shaped by the influence of religious fundamentalism, zealotry, and imperialism—both from Christian and Islamic persuasions. We already referenced one notable example in previous pages. In the interview with Godwin, he asserts that "I cannot imagine the religion I was brought up in having such complete contempt for human lives. And yet these are supposed to be the world religions. So that's why I consider myself rather fortunate that I've been able to see what other religions had to offer." Here, Soyinka is referring to a recent massacre in Federal Polytechnic College in the city of Mubi in northeastern Nigeria, in which 50 Nigerian students became victims of religious violence. The Islamic religious militant group, known as Boko Haram, located in Northern Nigeria, orchestrated the crime in the first week of October in 2012. Initially, Boko Haram was linked with the al-Qaeda; both groups worked collaboratively to carry a similar mission: the spreading of the Gospel of Islamic Jihadism, and the total devotion to Islam and the will of Allah. We suggest that Boko Haram should be understood as a *réseau radical* ("radical network") with both religious and political leanings; thus, it is a religious-political group.

Soyinka, having denounced the murderous orgy of Boko Haram, argues that it is actually "the psychopaths of faith" who are guilty of bringing disrepute to the religion of Islam, whose mission, in the name of their prophet, constitutes the "commission of crimes that revolt our very humanity."[21] He deprecates his own country Nigeria for contributing to "international terrorism of the religious brand."[22] While he is unquestionably an enthusiast Nigerian Patriot, he is not a passive public intellectual and social critic.

In the same interview with Godwin, Soyinka also indicates that to practice one's religion is a human right and "religion is also freedom of expression." He consents that religious proselytization is a form of religious freedom, and should not be taken away from religions and religious adherents. However, he condemns the outrageous and callous method that accompanies religious conversion in order to acquire new converts. "People want to express themselves spiritually. And they also exercise the right to try and persuade others into their own system of belief. Those nations that say it's a crime to preach your religion are making a terrible mistake. All they're doing is driving underground other forms of spiritual intuitions and practices." The religious experience should be viewed as a distinctively interpretive mode of the human life, and one's inclination toward faith should be regarded as an exercise of "cognitive freedom;" the later may be expressed in the public sphere.[23]

The spread of dangerous religious ideologies in the world could result in the spread of human violence and suffering, even to the point of death. It is within this context Soyinka urged the eradication of all religions in society. In an unapologetic tone, he states to Godwin, "If religion was to be taken away from the world completely, including the one I grew up with, I'd be one of the happiest people in the world. My only fear is that maybe something more terrible would be invented to replace it, so we'd better just get along with what there is right now and keep it under control." Soyinka's clarion call for "the end of faith" should be studied in its rightful context and the history of religious violence in his own native land and in the modern world. Soyinka is not an anti-religion critic, but a fervent critic of religious terrorism and fanaticism. In various occasions in his writings, he does affirm the positive role of religion in society and the therapeutic and comforting aspect of faith in this life of uncertainty and despair. It is of the African traditional religions and spirituality that he writes in a more positive light. As many people would agree, a life without any religious commitment is a life of spiritual unbalance.

In 1991, Wole Soyinka delivered the inaugural lecture in the Archbishop Olufosoye Lecture Series at the University of Ibadan entitled "The Credo of Being and Nothingness." In this seminal public address, Soyinka reflects theoretically and philosophically on the question of religion and its relevance in both private and public sphere. He also discusses his personal attitude toward various religious worldviews and traditions. He commences the lecture by recounting an early religious experience which he underwent as a child in his attempt to grasp the theological concept of "emptiness" or "nothingness" as narrated in the creation story in the Book of Genesis in the Hebrew Bible. The adjectives "formless" and "empty" (or "void") are used literally in the referenced text to describe the formative state of heavens and the earth after God has created them: "In the beginning God created the heavens and the earth. [2] Now the earth was formless and empty, darkness was over the surface of the deep, and the Spirit of God was hovering over the waters" (Gen. 1:1–2). Soyinka thoughtfully contemplates on the mystery of the creation narrative and the idea of theistic creationism, which challenge the theory of evolution and Big Bang:

> I do not claim to know what has been the experience of others but, as a child, I found myself frequently indulging in a rather exotic mental exercise. It was an exercise which originated from my attempts to come to concrete terms with the Christian myth of the creation of the world. In the beginning, claim the Christian scriptures, there was Void. Emptiness. My imagination insisted on conjuring up this primeval state and ended up by evolving this quite logical exercise: I would shut my eyes, shut off my mind, then try to enter that primal state of nothingness which the world would have been, before the creation of anything, animate or inanimate. It became quite a compulsive indulgence. I found myself impelled by a curiosity to experience the absolute state of non-being, of total void—no trees, no rocks, no skies, no other beings, not even I.[24]

This peculiar childhood experience of Soyinka clearly shows his early interest in religion and curiosity in matters of theology and philosophy. Soyinka's "exotic mental exercise" also demonstrates his previous attempt to understand precisely the rhetorical language of the first of all Christian theology—the doctrine of creation—and how God relates to the world he had created. Traditional Christian belief maintains the notion of *creatio ex nihilo* by divine fiat. God created the universe out of nothing! Orthodox Christianity affirms that God is the Creator of all things: both visible and invisible, spiritual and corporeal.

As a result of speculative imagination, Soyinka would orient his mind to "experience the absolute state of non-being," and comparatively, if we might infer, he would be compelled to seek the "One" who had brought to existence "the absolute state of total void and emptiness." Soyinka confessed that as an adult, he has moved beyond his elementary religious experiences to embrace a more robust religious and intellectual vision of the world. The adult Wole Soyinka was able "to construct complex philosophical and religious systems, in which all material life, including all those dynamic processes for the reproduction of life which in fact constitute our social consciousness or value of being, are actually conceived as a programmed reversion towards that very state of nothingness, the primal zero."[25] Soyinka has subscribed to a complex worldview-system that could be phrased radical theistic humanism and generous tolerance informed by the Yoruba religious culture and cosmology, and the Enlightenment humanism of the West. This attitude shows Soyinka's intellectual openness to bring Africa and the West in close conversation in matters of thought, faith, and practice.

The human experience in faith is a phenomenon that experiences change, transformation, and is unendingly evolving. Soyinka's "mature religious experience" would entail the interrogation of (and to a certain degree the renunciation of all) his formative religious beliefs and theological confessions. Some critics have advanced the idea that Soyinka has also rejected theism all together to embrace a robust non-theistic humanism worldview. We disagree with this conclusion. We suggest that Soyinka's new experiences (and continuous religious adventures) are still in line with traditional theistic humanism; but, it is a non-Christian theism clothed in the Yoruba religious tradition and spirituality.

Perhaps, the recorded passage in Soyinka's *Ake* is intended to signal his religious shift, the shipwreck of his faith: "The period of faith is gone. There was faith among our early Christians, real faith, not just church-going and hymn-singing. Faith. *Igbagbo*. And it is out of that faith that real power comes . . . "[26] As a student in middle school, he also reports his initial doubt about the credibility of the Jonah story in the Bible, and the myth that Jonah was swallowed by a big fish and stayed in its belly for three days: "Until the school teacher turned it into a fairy stale. Swallowed and sealed up in a whale's belly! It did not sound wholly improbable but it did belong in a world of fables, of the imagination, of Aladdin's lamp and Open Sesame."[27] He also doubted the efficacy of Christian prayer and that of her mother in particular:

> I had long lost faith in the efficacy of Wild Christian's prayers. There were several of her wards over whom she prayed night and day. She took them into the church and prayed over them, found any excuse, any opportunity at all to drag them before the altar and pray over them. They continued to steal, lie, fight or do whatever it was she prayed against.[28]

For the young Soyinka, God simply does not answer prayers: "The scale of such perversity, it seemed must beyond the remedy of prayers since the two had the entire church to themselves and God was not being distracted by other voices from the same direction."[29] Accordingly, the inference could be articulated as such: if human prayers do not matter to God or moves his heart to act in good faith, then he's not involved in human affair and unresponsive to human needs and suffering. In addition, as Soyinka himself has remarked, humanism was a prevalent attitude among the Ake people: "We all pray that our children go farther than we did, and we try to help God answer our prayers."[30] In other words, it is man who works his own miracles, not God. Religious syncretism was an acceptable practice among the people in Abeokuta. Unwavering faithfulness to a singular deity and resolute commitment to one particular religious tradition or system was a rare thing to find among the Yoruba people: "Our society definitely believes in God—or gods. That means we also believe in what we call an act of God—which is the same as reverses of human expectations."[31] Yet, there were many Yoruba skeptics, but not atheists.[32] Wole Soyinka belongs to the first category.

Perhaps, the most descriptive and illustrative passage that chronicles Soyinka's shipwreck of faith and radical agnosticism revealed in the interesting character of Komi—a young University student at the University College in Ibadan—is incorporated in his memoir *Ibadan*:

> How it all came about, he no longer remembered. He only recalled that the usual notice had gone up for articles for the school magazine, and he had resolved to set down, in continuous form, arguments that he often held with Komi, Chris, and sometimes even the quiet Dipo over what had become the major concern of his private reflections: did God exist? He had not yet come to a definition of his convictions, fluctuating as he did between a feeling that rejected the existence of such an omnipotent being, or at least the need to worship and bow before his unseen presence, and a fear of the deeply ingrained penalties that would attend such a denial, were to be wrong . . . With every reflection on the phenomena around him, causality began to replace all notion of miracle or divine origin. And yet he found that he clung deeply to evidence of mystery, to the mysterious, to the existence of a plane that remained non-physical.
>
> He no longer made a pretense of exploring the religious tracts still dutifully sent by his father; they did not contribute anything to his sense of wellbeing, his moral sense drew nourishment elsewhere, from other books that he read, from his continuing assessment of the lessons imparted from childhood . . . [33]

It is evident in the text that Komi embodies the religious ideas of cynicism and uncertainty of Soyinka. Soyinka went through a crisis of faith as a University student. As the character Komi, he doubted God's existence, and progressively abandoned the Christian teachings of his parents about morality, truth, and the meaning of life. Ultimately, he also rejected the infallibility and credibility of the Bible, discarded the divine origin of miracles, and interrogated the rationality of his parents' biblical principles on life and faith issues.

> Every day, the tracts seemed to grow even more pretentious, unctuous and even ludicrous. He could not see how the setting of a weekly homily could affect one's conduct for a week. His interest in the bible waned; there was literature that spoke more pertinently to him, that engaged his moral apprehension in more challenging, more enlarging ways. The chapel services became hollow and meaningless . . . at the time he could not even begin to move beyond the question: Where is God? Show me. Up there, I know he is not. So, if he is, show me where?
> But it was worship, regimented worship that first lost all conviction. Without any help from him, the Sunday worship simply divorced itself from what he had come to experience as spirpitualty. As for the sermons, they existed on a plane of smug repetitiousness; he failed to see what new perceptions on life, on morality or virtues his father, and all those excitable debaters who gathered around him, could really claim to draw from them, yet by common agreement they appeared to assess them in all seriousness.[34]

In the University lecture previously mentioned above, Soyinka confesses unreservedly that "I am not a Christian."[35] He considers himself as an individual who has raised himself "as an experimenting spiritualist of nothingness since childhood, graduating, under prison conditions, into even deeper illumination into the profundities of nothingness."[36] Accordingly, we can conclude that the young Soyinka was an agnostic in the making and was not committed to any creed, spiritual dogmatism, or religious tradition. In fact, in the same lecture, Soyinka references the ideas and writings of the esteemed eleventh-century Persian poet, philosopher, scientist, and agnostic Omar Khayyám in order to avow his own agnostic orientation to maters of religious belief and epistemology: "To be free from belief and unbelief is my religion."[37]

Our modern world is marked by perpetual contestation and rivalry between religions and religious extremists. Religious zealots proclaim boldly that they have the ultimate truth, and that their religion is the only acceptable path to God. It is in this perspective that Soyinka invites us to consider Khayyam before considering the non-negotiable demands of religion upon our lives. Khayyam looked at all religious traditions with the eye of a cynic, and for him, the demands that religion places on individuals are impractical and untenable. It is from this vantage point that Soyinka, who views skepticism as a form of human virtue in the tradition of humanism, advises that we take note of

> Khayyam's humility, which stresses the uncertainty of knowledge and the imperfectability of the human mind as instrument for grapping the ineffable,

embraces virtues that are often obscured by his unapologetic celebration of *joi de vivre*, by his Epicurean vitality. These virtues are however of crucial relevance to our global religious plight, and we do worse than resurrect such questing tempers of mind from centuries' neglect. Omar Khayyam's sense of inner harmony, translated into imperishable lines, may be the kind of music needed to rescue from the cacophony of the warring sects and religious extremism.[38]

Speaking about his own country, he references Khayyam as a possible prognosis to the future of religious conflict in Nigeria: "I often think that he (Khayyam) should be living in this age, and in this country. He was dubbed a heretic by some, but that is always a subjective point of view and what this nation needs with its current rash of possessed born-again Christians on the one hand, and their partners in Islamic extremism on the other, is a corrective presence of an Omar Khayyam, preferably in large closes."[39] Soyinka qualifies this statement with another one: "The poetry of Omar Khayyam and, of course, its pantheistic philosophy, its sublime iconoclasm, are infinitely more humanistic than any scriptures which tolerate, indeed promote the denial of human value or the sanctity of human life."[40] On the other hand, in promoting an agnostic worldview or orientation to life in general, Soyinka urges that "Our institutions need to promote extra-curricular studies of the agonistics, for the terrain of learning should be that paradox of 'the desert and the foundation,' its ideal denizen the 'fainting Traveler' pursuing the 'dimp glimpse' of Truth."[41] Soyinka's revolutionary agnosticism, framed within radical humanism, is more pronounced in this provocative statement: "Erase that temple! Demolish that mosque! Obliterate that cathedral! Flatten that shrine!"[42]

Soyinka's clarion call to extinguish worship centers should not be quickly interpreted as a demonstration of (his) religious intolerance or bigotry. Rather, this puzzling attitude means to counter the spread of religious extremism and discourage religious imperialism: "Each major religion and even sect within the same religion appears periodically incapable of finding its own centre except by the act of reducing the other in some form or the other to nothing."[43] Although his target audience was Nigerian religious zealots, the moral of his provocation might be applicable cross-culturally and transnationally. Unquestionably, the human plague we call religious fanaticism has no boundary. Soyinka's religious sensibility is his impenitent revolutionary agnosticism inspired by Yoruba philosophy of religious inclusivity and tolerance.

To recapitulate, Soyinka has abandoned his Anglican faith to cling to a broad-minded worldview and philosophy: the indigenous religious tradition and humanism of the Yoruba people. He has rejected the doctrine of the absolute unity (oneness) of God championed in Christian and Islamic theology to embrace a more elastic, less-robust, and non-dogmatic concept of God.

In addition to his questioning of the legitimacy of religious exclusivism, he has rejected the idea of divine revelation and the notion of "divinely-inspired Scriptures," two cardinal doctrines of the Abrahamic religions: Judaism, Christianity, and Islam. Nontheistic humanist philosopher Sam Harris has brilliantly underscored the possible dangers and consequences of non-progressive orientation to religion to scientific inquiry and human development:

> Anyone who wants to understand the world should be open to new facts and new augments, even on subjects where his or her views are well established. Similarly, anyone truly interested in morality—in the principles of behavior that allow people to flourish—should be open to new evidence and new arguments that bear upon questions of happiness and suffering. Clearly, the chief enemy of open conservation is dogmatism in all its form. Dogmatism is a well-recognized obstacle to scientific reasoning; and yet, because scientists have been reluctant even to imagine that they might have something prescriptive to say about values, dogmatism is still granted remarkable scope on questions of both truth and goodness under the banner of religion.[44]

In addition, Philosopher of religion John Hicks in his powerful text *An Interpretation of Religion* articulates an epistemological framework that cautious us about the nature of certainty in matters properly designated religious. In particular, he projects that things of religious value possess inherent ambiguity, fluidity, and elasticity. He establishes the relationship between the universe that exhibits a condition of orderly ambiguity and the paradoxes of the religious life:

> It seems, then, that the universe maintains its inscrutable ambiguity. In some aspects it invites whilst in others it repels a religious response. It permits both a religious and a naturalist faith, but haunted in each case by a contrary possibility that can never be exorcised. Any realistic analysis of religious belief and experience, and any realistic defense of the rationality of religious conviction, must therefore start with this situation of systematic ambiguity.[45]

Soyinka seems to hold a similar position to that of Hicks and ascribes to Harris's viewpoint about the dynamics between religion and science. Supposedly, as religion, science does not provide the absolute answer to human uncertainties or possess the absolute truth; as science, religion may provide some meaning to life. In various ways, science and religion can be said compatible—as both claim to improve society and enhance human relations in the modern world. Further, in various ways, both science and religion provide ways of knowing about the universe, ourselves, and God himself.

THE NATURE OF RELIGION

While religion is broadly construed as a neutral phenomenon on a global scale, in its ambiguous role, it can be used as a vehicle to foster good or bad, and to inflict pain on people or alleviate global suffering. On one hand, Soyinka understands that the misuse of religion could aggravate the human condition in the world.[46] In this line of reasoning, religion could be interpreted as a global crisis. On the other hand, he deduces that "the positive role of religious symbols as spiritual and ethical reminders in the consciousness of youthful minds at all times and as a corrective mechanism when one might be on the verge of misconduct."[47] In the subsequent paragraphs, the critical reader will quickly detect the intellectual tension in Soyinka's religious discourse.

Most scholars of religion consent that religion affects "not just our social, political, and economic conflicts, but the very meanings we find in our lives."[48] Hent de Vries in *Religion and Violence* has remarked that "Religion is crucial to the reassessment of recent debates concerning identity and self-determination, the modern nation-state and multiculturalism, liberal democracy and immigration, globalization and the emergence of new media, the virtualization of reality and the renegotiation of the very concept of the 'lifeworld,' to say nothing of the technologies of 'life.'"[49] Steve Bruce in *Politics & Religion* declares that "By binding a people together under a shared God, a common cosmology and a common morality, religion creates order and stability and its rituals create social cohesion. By promising to the pious poor rewards in the next life, it reconciles them to their fate in this one and thus discourages them from rebelling against their condition."[50]

Moreover, John Hicks in *God Has Many Names* asserts that the realm of religious experience and belief entail "our response to a transcendent divine reality or realities. It is the conviction, in other words, that religion is not, as a totality, illusion and self-deception."[51] Soyinka, however, has argued that religion is about humanity's pursuit of the divine; therefore, religion is "evidently entrenched in the human psyche."[52] Soyinka also advances the idea that the ultimate and highest religious feeling or experience is union and intimacy with God "in present existence or in afterlife."[53] While he recognizes the uniqueness of every religion, Soyinka explains that religious conflicts arise precisely because all religions possess distinctively inherent attributes, and "perhaps this is one of those instances where variety is not so much the spice of life as the trigger of strife.[54] Karen Armstrong articulates an alternative viewpoint that religions are antagonistic toward one another because they ostensibly share many characteristics:

> Like Judaism, and Islam, Christianity had an inherent leaning toward violence, despite the pacifism of Jesus. All three religions are historically and theologi-

cally related and all worship the same God. All three traditions are dedicated in some way to love and benevolence and yet all three have developed a pattern of holy war and violence that is remarkably similar and which seems to surface from some deep compulsion that is inherent in this tradition of monotheism, and the worship of only one God.[55]

If "the absolutism of religion has been revealed especially in the notion of cosmic war,"[56] is it possible then to prevent religious warfare in this age of religious violence and terrorism? Soyinka finds great promises in the tolerant, adaptive, and pluralistic nature of African traditional religions and the "secular gods" of the Yoruba people. African deities could potentially contribute to human peace and cooperation.

> What we must pursue, therefore, is not a competitive, bruising arena for the claims of ideology or religion but an open marketplace of both ideas and faiths. It is within this context, without any ambiguity, that the Orisa and their body of divine precepts, Ifa, prove of great humanistic value in the realm of religion. As quest, as the principle of spiritual enquiry, Ifa exemplifies this field of accommodation for all seekers, under no matter what structure of belief. This ancient religion that we have co-opted as a guide into our exploration of a noninterfering order of faith and spirituality proposes that "warfare between religions need not be. Its very nature protects it from the bellicose instinct that leads followers of other beliefs to defend even the most trivial annotation of their doctrinal text with their lives or, more accurately, with the lives of others, conveniently designated infidels, unbelievers, apostates, enemies of God, and other charitable epithets . . . Humanity is better served by the adoption of secularized deities than by those other gods of undoubtedly entrancing liturgies that evoked as control zones on humanity, tyrannized over by morals, no different from ourselves.[57]

On one hand, Soyinka would have us to believe that religion in general is the source of human suffering and violence in the world. On the other hand, he presents the Yoruba religious tradition (another form of religious expression) as a possible solution to the human predicament and the problem of religious tolerance in the world. This conflict is foreseeable in his philosophy of religion. Consider this important paragraph that reveals the democratic and loving nature of the Orisa:

> Religion, or profession of faith, cannot serve as the common ground for human coexistence except of course by the adoption of coercion as a principle and, thus, the manifestation of its corollary—hypocrisy—an outward conformism that is dictated by fear, by a desire for preferment, or indeed, the need for physical survival. In the end, the product is conflict, and the destruction of cultures. Let this be understood by the champions of theocracies where religion and ideology meet and embrace. Orisa admonishes them: you will not bring the world even close to the edge of combustion. The essence of Orisa is

the antithesis of tyranny, bigotry, and dictatorship—what greater gift than this respect, this spirit of accommodation, can humanity demand from the world of the spirit?

Thus, for all seekers after the peace and security of true community, and the space of serenity that enables the quest after truth, pleading for understanding from the Orisa for this transgression of their timeless scorn of proselytizing, we urge yet again the simple path that travelled from the soil of the Yoruba across the African landmass to continuous nations, across the hostile oceans to the edge of the world in the Americas—*Go to the Orisa, learn from the Orisa, and be wise.*[58]

Admittedly, Soyinka wants to proselytize individuals to the Yoruba faith and spirituality. It also appears that he is expressing a particular brand of religious exceptionalism—a thesis he will refute—committing the similar intellectual transgression of the Christians and Muslims whom he fiercely opposes? Perhaps, Soyinka is unable to reconcile intellectually this internal tension and rhetorical ambivalence—within himself. Is he being impartial? Is he demonstrating religious favoritism? Is he a genuine religious inclusivist and relativist? The subsequent paragraphs will shed further light concerning these pivotal matters.

In the Olufosoye Lecture referenced in the first section of the essay, Soyinka's own religious incredulity impels him to perform a comparative analysis of some of the shared concepts in Christianity, Islam, and Buddhism. To put it another way, he is interested in the scientific comparative method of religion. The attempt here is to harmonize & reconcile these faiths by way of establishing similarities and doctrinal or ideological connections. At this point, the subject matter is not what divides religions, but it is their sheer common traits or characteristics, and what we can take from each religious tradition to cultivate ecumenical understanding between people of different religious persuasions; this method aims at improving the human condition in the world through genuine interfaith conversations.

Soyinka provides a detailed description about these shared concepts found in the referenced World religions. It is important to reproduce his thought here in order for us to grasp clearly his thinking on the subject matter.

> What Christians and moslems share with Buddhism is not so much Nirvana as its universalizes state—Mahapralayi. This expression offers a loose distinction which I had better quality. I do not deny that there are states of individual contemplation in Christianity and Islam which approach the ideal of Nirvana. Certainly some of the fundamentalist sects in either religion indulge in this exercise of intensive inward dissolution which parallels the Buddhist Nirvana . . . The Universal Day of Judgment, guaranteed by both, is the concept I can propose which comes closest to the condition to universal nothingness, the in-folding of the world as we know it into its original womb of darkness, or

more accurately, non-darkness and non-light. The main differentiation between Mahapralayi and Day of Judgment is however a crucial, even cheerful one. The material world we know disappears, in the latter case, but it is revived on a different plane, as Paradise, Purgatory or Hell.[59]

Soyinka admits that mutual reciprocity and interdependence among the world's great faiths is not a matter of intellectual contestation. Despite the noticeable common theologies, shared rituals and ideologies within these religions, Soyinka points out that some traditions remain ignorant "of other systems of beliefs whether as philosophies, religions, or worldviews."[60] Secondly, such religions like Christianity and Islam, "that have been affected, or infected by aspects of other beliefs, and religious practices, have failed to grasp the essence of those other faiths which constitutes 'impurities' within their own spiritual blood-stream."[61] Thirdly, he laments that the so-called revelatory religions "prefer to persecute manifestations of such realities, to excommunicate or indeed exterminate them, thereby depriving themselves of the most rudimentary knowledge of the other."[62] Fourthly, Soyinka recommends that religions that have disseminated elaborate beliefs or fantasies through violence "spread unspeakable cruelties on people in the name of conversion, or the preservation of the purity of sheer spiritual institutions should be allowed to exist in their own right, but in their own place."[63]

As can be observed, Soyinka's fierce criticism on religion is not without viable merit or historical justification. His harsh assessment does not, however, earn him the title "anti-religion critic." He himself illuminates this point in the lecture:

> I must not be misunderstood. I extol, indeed, I partake with creative and humane enlargement, in the inherent and productive values of all religions, their monumental legacies to the world, their piety and unflagging spirit of the search for truth. I acknowledge that the word would be a much poorer place without the phenomenon of religion. I do not refer here merely to their architectural and artistic legacies but even to the inspirational value of their scriptures, the lyricism in which they are frequently couched, and the intellectual challenges of their exegeses.[64]

RELIGION AND THE SOCIAL ORDER

Soyinka has claimed that religious exclusivism ("exclusivist dicta") "is the most insidious of all such . . . whose stridency both historically and in contemporary times, has taken on aggressive and territorially rapacious proportions."[65] (Here, Soyinka does not assert that cults produce religious terror, but they're certainly not immune from it). He avers that the exclusivist dicta of religion are "the most persistent credo that militates against the evolution of a harmonious, all embracing human community."[66] The dictum of religious exclusivism is framed within this linguistic code: "'I believe, therefore, I am.' 'You do not believe, therefore you are.'"[67] This unwavering pronouncement has not only produced religious alienation, but also human estrangement and existential isolation. The crisis and consequences of religious exclusivism is emphasized further in this paragraph:

> the believers of every so-called major religion will claim that they do not deny humanity to 'unbelievers' but, history, even contemporary history, gives them the lie. The dictum is embedded in their daily pronouncements, their daily activities, exhortations, disseminated precepts, social attitudes etc., etc., but, most critically and dangerously, even in their political acts and pronouncements. When all else fails, and even before all else has been attempted, it supplies the fuel for the machinery of tyrannical political schemes, social advantages and other forms of opportunism. "I believe, therefore, I am." "You disbelieve, therefore you are not"; therefore, you count for nothing. You are subhuman. You are outside the pale of humanity, outside the concept of community.[68]

Contrary to Soyinka's thesis, Harold Netland in *Dissonant Voices* has argued that at the heart of religious pluralism is "the epistemological confusion in much of the current debate lie some erroneous assumptions about the nature of religious truth."[69] Soyinka closes the Archbishop Olufosoye Lecture Series by urging his Nigerian audience to reevaluate African traditional religions against the imported religious practices and beliefs, and to weigh African spirituality against the foreign forms of spirituality practiced in the continent; yet, these religions, such as Islam and Christianity, are fully integrated in African religions. Because of the openness and fluidity of African religions, Soyinka projects that they might be a possible solution to the dilemma of religious violence in the world.

> For the rest, I wish only to exhort you: study the spirituality of this continent. As in all things, selectiveness is the key. To limit myself to that with which I am on familiar grounds, I say to you: go to the *orisa*, learn from them and be wise. The religion of the *orisa* does not permit, in tenets, liturgy, catechism or practice, that pernicious dictum: "I believe, therefore I am." Nowhere will you find the sheerest skein of reasoning in that direction to human self-apprehension. Obviously, therefore, you will not find its corollary: "You do not believe, therefore you are not." *Orunmila* does not permit it. *Obatala* cannot conceive of it. Ogun will take up arms against it. No one *odu* of IFA so much as suggests it. It is not weakness in the character of this religion however, it is not even tolerance. It is simply—understanding. Wisdom. An intuitive grasp of the complexity of the human mind, and a true sense of the infinite potential of the universe.[70]

In a different set of lectures entitled "Climate of Fear" delivered at the Royal Institution in London in March 2004, Soyinka discusses the content of faith and analyses the integrative elements of religion. As the title of the lectures indicates, the phenomenon of fear is assumed to be the representative feeling of religion. Soyinka does not come to the general conclusion that the starting point of religion is fear—as many scholars have traditionally maintained. On the contrary, he insists that religious zealots produce a climate of fear in order to carry out their political agendas. Corey Robin in his important work *Fear: The History of a Political Idea* connects political fear with the rule of the law and attests that "Political fear is supposed to teach us the worth of specific political values. The fear of civil war, for instance, is supposed to breed a respect for the rule of law, the fear of totalitarianism an appreciation for liberal democracy, the fear of fundamentalism support for tolerance and pluralism."[71] Secondly, Soyinka establishes a close rapport between religious fanaticism and secularism. In both worldviews, the place for tolerance and of dissent in social interaction is ambiguous.[72] Nonetheless, he highlights some wide dissimilarity or differences between the religious order and the secular order. He posits that the differences in both systems may help us to appreciate the importance of human freedom; in a sense, it could be argued that both orders could potentially be seen as a threat to human freedom, flourishing, and subjectivity

As a humanist, Soyinka seems to give prominence to secularism. He undermines any possibility of religion to contribute meaningfully to human freedom, peace, and the common good—with the exception of the Yoruba tradition. In his attempt to differentiate the two orders—the religious and the secular— he explains with clarity the constituent elements of each one. Let us consider his assessment on the latter:

> Secular ideology derives its theories from history and the material world. The mind has therefore learned to pause occasionally and reflect on the processes that link the material world to doctrines that derive from or govern it, to review changes in such a world, test theories against old and new realities—be they economic, cultural, industrial, or even environmental. The dynamic totality of the real world is given rational space.[73]

Complementarity, Soyinka has remarked:

> Within a secular dispensation, even under the most rigid totalitarian order, its underpinning ideology—that, the equivalent of theology—remains open to contestation. Open questioning may be suppressed, open debate may be restricted or prohibited by the state or the party of power, but the functioning of the mind, its capacity for critique—even self-criticism—never ceases.[74]

Hence, two characteristics stand out in the secular framework: rationality and self-criticism. By contrast, under the theocratic order,

> One that derives its authority not from theories that are elicited from the material conditions of society but from the secret spaces of revelation, this disposition of the mind toward alternative concepts or variants is next to impossible. Curiosity succumbs to fear, often masquerading as pious submission. The theocratic order derives its mandate from the unknown.[75]

Soyinka explains further that

> Only a chosen few are privileged to have penetrated the workings of the mind of the unknown, whose constitution—known as the Scriptures—they and they alone can interpret. The fanatic that is born of this dogmatic structure of the ineffable, religion, is the most dangerous being on earth.[76]

The problem arises especially when one fails to respond positively to the totality of religious fanaticism, which could result in extended discrimination, and to the point that "all are pronounced guilty who do not share this mind-set of the fanatic, or who dare propose a different worldview from that which motivates it."[77] Religious extremism is grounded in "the philosophy of elitism, a philosophy of the Chosen versus the Rest."[78] How should we then respond collectively to religious fundamentalism, and the global menace of religious fanatics?

Soyinka provides some helpful recommendations:

> We must seek in the common denominator that unites the opposite extremes of beliefs and ideologies but also breeds and nurtures the fanatic, intolerant mind. While we are engaged on that quest, we, the Rest, in whatever aspect of belief we are thus defined, must either lay our necks tamely on this versatile execution block or imaginatively pursue remedial action. This involves, certainly, eradicating those conditions that serve as ready recruitment agencies—poverty, political injustice, and other forms of social alienation—but, even more crucially, demonstrating in an equally determined, structured way our right, indeed our duty, to implement strategies of self-protection, making it abundantly clear that the other of doctrine of the Chosen is intolerable to humanity. To do otherwise is to condone the doctrine that moves so arrogantly from *I am right, you are wrong* to its fatal manifestation as *I am right; you are dead*.[79]

Next, Soyinka implies that generally, religion has not improved the human condition nor has it contributed anything constructive to human progress and the advancement of universal civilizations:

> All we can be certain of (because it is clearly provable) is that the proliferation of grandiose cathedrals, basilicas, temples, mosques, shrines, and other places of worship throughout the global landscape has not perceptibly improved the living conditions or moral sensibilities of the large part of humanity, if we judge by both the physical conditions of the populace where these architectural caryatids are situated and their social conduct.[80]

While the track record of religion is shameful and depressing, the effective use of religion could potentially lead to a more fruitful life and human interaction in the world. Soyinka and most nontheistic humanists have underestimated the value of religion in public and personal life. Contrary to Soyinka's negative discourse on religion, religion has the potentiality to (1) cultivate the whole person, (2) provide people with a view of the world and a view of themselves, (3) provide mankind with moral values by which to live, (4) give food for spiritual hunger, and (5) show people their limitations and the need for God.[81] Furthermore, Soyinka has belittled the work of religion to alleviate poverty in the modern world and improve the social order. In China, for example, Buddhism was used politically as an instrument to unify various political parties, and people of various ethnic and class background that were once divided. Similarly, in India, under the leadership of Gandhi, Hinduism was instrumental in solidifying the Indian population against their British colonizers and oppressors; Hinduism has helped India become a free and independent nation from the British rule.

It is doubtful about any historical intervention or instance of any religion in human history aiming at alleviating poverty in the world. He is also cynical about the instrumental role of religion in fostering human harmony and collaboration among people; as he pronounces forcefully:

> It is difficult for instance to recall that there were times when religion was a harmonizing factor even between communities of different faiths, that a spiritual richness pervaded daily existence no matter whether it came from the Moslem, traditional, or Christian social and religious structures and observances. The use of which religion is put today (and we speak here not merely of extremists but of government complicity) often translates directly into politics, both local and national.[82]

Because of the supposedly-ineffectiveness of religion in society, Soyinka disapproves the use of religion in the public sphere and the political arena. He posits that "The world would of course be a simpler space to contend if only religion kept within the domain of the spiritual."[83] For him, the city of God is antagonistic to the city of man. These two worlds are not compatible; they belong to different domains and are opposite poles. It is true that religion is intertwined with power politics, and it "is an order that remains incapable of remaining within a private zone that does not translate into *power*—as distinct from *guidance*—over others."[84] The most frightening and challenging matter about the workings of religion for Soyinka is expressed in this direct language: "the incursion of religion into the secular domain, appropriating the provinces of ethics, mores, and social conduct—and even the sciences—guarantees the clerical dominance of the total field of play."[85] The anxiety between religion and politics is "the intrusion of political opportunism into the workings of religious zealotry, a common enough marriage of convenience that gives birth to monstrosities."[86] Evidently, "the world of the fanatic is one and it cuts across all religions, ideologies, and vocations."[87]

In addition, the crisis of public religion is that "piety has become equated with ostentatious religionism and even elevated, in certain recent instances, to the status of state policies by public servants whose private practices would hardly bear the right test of their own religious precepts."[88] In the case of Nigeria, for example, Soyinka has become profoundly discontent with various attempts by the State "to introduce religious separatism through the uniforms of schools pupils, and hospital nurses."[89] This tentative effort would problematize the role of religion in public education and deprive students "of that phase of humanistic oneness to which they are entitled, as an essential dimension of their positive knowledge of human society and the development of their sense of community."[90] Soyinka projects that the implementation of religion in state-sponsored institutions and programs could potentially be used as a pernicious device to discriminate and defer collective unity and human solidarity.

Soyinka puts forth the uncontested idea that religion has the potentiality to engender global suffering and collective alienation. He alerts his readers of the possible danger of Muslim fundamentalists and Christian enthusiasts. To recapitulate, he does not speak positively about Christianity and Islam for "they represent only a part of the many global strains of spiritual adhesion that constantly threaten to bring the world to that presumably blissful condition of nothingness, or Mahapralayi."[91] While religious fanatics demand total devotion to their faith, submission is the bedrock of all religion, including African traditional religions. The terrifying matter with the religious zealot is that he is "one who creates a Supreme Being, or Supreme Purpose, in his or her own image, then carries out the orders of that solipsistic device that commands from within, in lofty alienation from, and utter contempt of, society and community."[92]

THE TRAP OF RELIGIOUS EXCLUSIVISM AND ABSOLUTISM

A similar concern with religious zealotry is its exclusive claim of ultimate truth and divine election, and its appeal to divine authority to segregate the world into two polarizing spheres of existence. Religious exclusivists, accordingly, claim to be the guardian of divine Truth on this earth; as Soyinka remarks candidly:

> The stillborn dogmatism of *I am right, you are wrong* has circled back since the contest of ideologies and once again attained its apotheosis of I am right; you are dead. The monologue of unilateralism constantly aspires the mantle of the Chosen and, of course, further dichotomizes the world, inviting us, on pain of consequences, to choose between "them" and "us."[93]

Soyinka interrogates the very premise which religious exclusivists and fanatics base their unqualified assertion of absolute truth and political correctness. For Soyinka, truth is relative, inclusive, and not absolute the same way there is no absolute and true or false religion. Pragmatist philosophy maintains "the notion that our belief might correspond with reality is absurd. Beliefs are simply tools for making one's way in the world."[94] In other words, there is no such a thing as value, but values. There is no such a thing as the truth, but truths. There is no such a thing as purpose, but purposes. There is no such a thing as revelation, but revelations. There is no such a thing as reality, but realities. It is subjective that remains the final authority. In a sophisticated philosophical essay, prominent African philosopher Kwasi Wiredu has brilliantly reasoned that "there is nothing called Truth as distinct from opinion."[95] Stressing the plurality of truth as much as human opinions, he makes the following observation:

> In the case of truth as in our previous case of "Reality," we must recognize the cognitive element of point of view as intrinsic to the concept of truth. Truth, then, is necessarily joined to the point of view, or better, truth is a view from some point; and there are as many truths as there are points of view . . . Truth and falsity are concepts whose whole essence consists simply in indicating the agreement or disagreement of one point of view with another, antecedent or anticipated . . . Whatever theory of truth holds or may come to hold the field, some people will continue to consider nonsensical what others embrace as wisdom . . . On the practical plane, then, the identification of truth with opinion may be interpreted as a prescription for open-mindedness. This quality of mind consists not in affecting uncertainty but in recognizing one's liability to error.[96]

Working from a different school thought, Harold Netland states that "Exclusivism presupposes that one can make accurate judgments about the truth or falsity of the major religions. But many today deny that it is possible to apply objective, nonarbitrary criteria in the assessment of various religious traditions."[97] Soyinka would agree with Wiredu and challenge Netland's position. Like Wiredu, Soyinka would assent that "The concept of absolute truth appears to have a tendency to facilitate dogmatism and fanaticism which lead, in religion and politics, to authoritarianism and, more generally, to obsession."[98] Nonetheless, Wiredu's conclusion may not be necessarily truthful and consequential.

We agree that each religious tradition has its distinctive system of ethic and value. Soyinka includes non-theistic religion and agnostics in the conversation. Soyinka's reflective questions encourage further inquiry into the puzzling nature and workings of religion:

> What does this mean for those billions of the world who are determined unbelieves? What does it mean for the world of Hindus, Buddhists, the Zo-

roastrias, the followers of Orisa, and a hundred of other faiths that routinely marginalized in the division of the world between two blood-stained behemoths of faith—the Islamic and the Judeo-Christian?[99]

CONCLUSION

As can be observed in our analysis in this chapter, Soyinka's general perspective on religion is not articulated in a positive light. It is shaped by a high degree of religious indecision or skepticism, and a philosophical worldview grounded on open tolerance and the improbability of knowledge and truth. Violence is the underlying concept he employs to describe all religious activities and transactions in this world. He remarks, "Violence appears to be the one constant in the histories of all the major religions of the world—a primitive aggressiveness, violence."[100] The alternative to religious violence is radical humanism which promotes (religious) tolerance, peace, community, understanding, and ecumenical dialogue. While Soyinka stresses the practice and presence of violence in the Abrahamic religions, ambiguously, their sacred texts both condemn and extol "holy hostility towards non-believers."[101] Second to violence is the notion of intolerance and fear, which are produced deliberately by all religious fanatics, zealots, or extremists. These elements constitute the negative effects of religion in both political and civil societies.

Soyinka's radical humanism is not without fault. While Soyinka's humanism is found helpful for interfaith dialogue, the recognition of religious difference is also crucial for understanding what sets the religions of the world apart from each other—an important matter he has overlooked in his analysis. Secondly, inclusive tolerance does not mean one has to undermine theological differences and doctrinal distinctions that exist between religions. Religious homogeneity does not, in fact, promote a peaceful life, and will not solve religious bigotry and violence in the modern world. In the final chapter in the book, we shall return to Soyinka's theory of radical humanism and how it could contribute to a better world. In the transition, let us now turn to his discourse on religious violence in the subsequent chapter.

NOTES

1. Soyinka, "Neo-Tarzanism: The Poetics of Pseudo-Tradition," in Soyinka, Art, *Dialogue, and Outrage*, 300–1. To learn more about Christian cultural imperialism and the rejection of traditional forms, and Christian re-consecration of theatrical forms, see Soyinka's critique of the movement, "Theatre in African Traditional Cultures: Survival Patterns," 134–146, in the same text mentioned in this footnote.
2. Soyinka, *Art, Dialogue, and Outrage*, 3001
3. "Wole Soyinka: 'If religion was taken away I'd be happy.'" *The Telegraph*. 12 Oct 2012. Accessed July 6, 2012. http://www.telegraph.co.uk/culture/hay-festival/9600954/Wole-Soyin-

ka-If-religion-was-taken-away-Id-be-happy.html. Wole Soyinka was the invited speaker to the Hay Festival in Mexico, which occurred in October 2012.
  4. Soyinka, *Of Africa*, 185.
  5. "Wole Soyinka: 'If religion was taken away I'd be happy.'"
  6. Soyinka, *Ibadan: The Penkelmes Years: A Memoir 1946–65*, 165.
  7. Soyinka, *You Must Set Forth at Dawn*, 6. In *Of Africa*, he refers to Ogun, "confessedly my adopted companion principle," 158.
  8. Gibbs, "Introduction," in James Gibbs, *Critical Perspectives on Wole Soyinka*, 3.
  9. Soyinka, *You Must Set Forth at Dawn*, 34, 44.
  10. Soyinka, Myth, *Literature and the African World*, 1–2.
  11. Gibbs, "Introduction," in James Gibbs, *Critical Perspectives on Wole Soyinka*, 3.
  12. Gikandi, "Introduction," in Soyinka, *Death and the King's Horseman*, viii.
  13. Ibid., xi.
  14. Soyinka, *Ibadan: The Penkelemes Years*, 166. He also remarks:

There did exist, he acknowledged, a territory of the ineffable, what, for want of a better term, he conceded to spirituality; it was an awareness of an essence in all things that transcended the mundane, but this he found present, in a more forceful yet unobtrusive way, in the orchard of Unter den Linden, in the voice of Paul Robeson singing the poem of William Blake . . .

  15. Soyinka, *You Must Set Forth at Dawn*, 46.
  16. Ibid., 46, 49, 112.
  17. Soyinka, "Theatre in African Traditional Cultures: Survival Patterns," in *Soyinka, Art, Dialogue, and Outrage*, 135.
  18. Ibid., 136.
  19. Harris, *The Moral Landscape*, 144.
  20. Dennett, *Breaking the Spell*, 12.
  21. Soyinka, "Psychopaths of Faith vs. The Muse of Irreverence,"13.
  22. Soyinka, *Of Africa*, 188.
  23. Netland, *Encountering Religious Pluralism*, 220.
  24. Soyinka, *Art, Dialogue, and Outrage*, 231.
  25. Ibid.
  26. Soyinka, *Ake: The Years of Childhood*, 7.
  27. Ibid., 64.
  28. Ibid., 105.
  29. Ibid.
  30. Soyinka, *Isara: A Voyage Around "Essay,"* 148.
  31. Ibid., " 35, 76.
  32. Ibid., " 45, 33.
  33. Soyinka, *Ibadan: The Penkelemes Years*, 165–6.
  34. Soyinka, *Ibadan: The Penkelemes Years*, 165–6.
  35. Soyinka, *Art, Dialogue, and Outrage*, 233.
  36. Ibid.
  37. Ibid., 236.
  38. Soyinka, *Art, Dialogue, and Outrage*, 237.
  39. Ibid., 234.
  40. Ibid., 236.
  41. Ibid., 237.
  42. Ibid.
  43. Ibid.
  44. Harris, *The End of Faith*, 22–3.
  45. Hicks, *Interpretation of Religion*, 124.
  46. Soyinka, *The Open Sore of a Continent*, 122.
  47. Soyinka, *Climate of Fear*, 116, 128. Further, Soyinka makes an important connection between spirituality and body, which he fails to explore further. He writes: "The provenance of faith is the soul and, by extension, the soul's material housing, the body itself." It would have been constructive has he illustrated the bond between faith, soul, and the body.

48. Dennett, *Breaking the Spell*, 14–5.
49. De Vries, *Religion and Violence*, xi.
50. Bruce, *Religion & Politics*, 10.
51. Hicks, *God Has Many Names*, 88.
52. Soyinka, *Of Africa*, 135.
53. Ibid., 132.
54. Ibid.
55. Armstrong, *Holy War: The Crusades and their Impact on Today's World*, 5–6.
56. Juergensmeyer, *Terror in the Mind of God*, 220.
57. Soyinka, *Of Africa*, 134–5.
58. Ibid., 168.
59. Soyinka, *Art, Dialogue, and Outrage*, 232.
60. Ibid., 238.
61. Ibid.
62. Ibid.
63. Ibid., 239–40.
64. Ibid., 240.
65. Soyinka, *Art, Dialogue, and Outrage*, 245.
66. Ibid.
67. Ibid.
68. Ibid.
69. Netland, *Dissonant Voices*, xi.
70. Soyinka, *Art, Dialogue, and Outrage*, 246.
71. Robin, *Fear: The History of a Political Idea*, 4.
72. Soyinka, *Climate of Fear*, 125.
73. Ibid., 126.
74. Ibid.
75. Ibid., 127.
76. Ibid.
77. Ibid., 128.
78. Ibid.
79. Ibid.
80. Soyinka, *The Open Sore of a Continent*, 112.
81. Mbiti, *Introduction to African Religion*, 198–201.
82. Ibid., 121.
83. Soyinka, *Climate of Fear*, 129.
84. Ibid.
85. Ibid.
86. Ibid., 130.
87. Ibid., 134.
88. Soyinka, *Art, Dialogue, and Outrage*, 234.
89. Ibid.
90. Ibid.
91. Ibid.
92. Soyinka, *Climate of Fear*, 134.
93. Ibid.
94. Harris, *The End of Faith*, 180.
95. Wiredu, *Philosophy and An African Culture*, 111.
96. Wiredu, *Philosophy and An African Culture*, 115–123.
97. Netland, *Dissonant Voices*, xi.
98. Wiredu, *Philosophy and An African Culture*, 122.
99. Soyinka, *Climate of Fear*, 135.
100. Soyinka, *Art, Dialogue, and Outrage*, 238.
101. Ibid.

Chapter Two

Against Violence

The Arrogance of Faith and Religious Imperialism

The Nigerian playwright, public intellectual, and humanist Wole Soyinka once announced, "Violence appears to be the one constant in the histories of all the major religions of the world—a primitive aggressiveness, violence." The objective of this chapter is to study Soyinka's response to violence and terror fueled by religious imperialism, fanaticism, and religious conviction. While religion in general plays a central role in Soyinka's creative writings, scholars have given limited attention to his engagement with faith in his nonfiction productions. Consequently, there exists both an intellectual and literary gap to bridge Soyinka's religious ideas expressed in his fictions and those he enunciated in his other writing. In response to religious imperialism and absolutism, this chapter argues that Soyinka relies heavily on the wisdom and principles of two worldviews and ideologies: African indigenous humanism and African traditional religion and spirituality. This idea is developed more full in the final two chapters of the book.

THE PROBLEM OF RELIGION: VIOLENCE AND FEAR

Like the human will, religion is an imaginative human enterprise that animates good and/or bad choices, generates constructive and/or destructive ideas or concepts that shape the human experience in this world. "Religion, however it is defined, involves a certain kind of attitude."[1] Immanuel Kant in Religion within the Limits of Reason Alone associates the freedom of choice to the disposition (Gesinnung) of the will (Willkür). The paragraph below briefly references this vital aspect of Kant's moral philosophy:

> The freedom for the will [Willkür] is a wholly unique nature in that an incentive can determine the will to an action only so far as the individual has incorporated it into his maxim (has made it the general rule in accordance with which he will conduct himself); only thus can an incentive, whatever it may be, coexist with the absolute spontaneity of the will [Willkür] (i.e. freedom).[2]

Like religion, the human will "is neither intrinsically good nor intrinsically evil; rather, it is the capacity by which we freely choose good or evil maxims."[3] Nonetheless, we should not equate religion with the "faculty of free spontaneous choice" (Willkür); religious choices, beliefs, or convictions are the outright expressions of the disposition of the will. Silber establishes an important connection between the will and disposition:

> The development of the [concept of Gesinnung] is, perhaps, the most important single contribution of the Religion to Kant's ethical theory, for by means of it he accounts for the continuity and responsibility in the free exercise of Willkür and for the possibility of ambivalent volition, as well as the basis for its complex assessment . . . The disposition [Gesinnung] is thus the enduring aspect of Willkür, it is Willkür considered in terms of the continuity and fullness of its free expression. It is the enduring pattern of intention that can be inferred from the many discrete acts of Willkür and reveals their ultimate motive.[4]

Another important feature in Kant's moral philosophy that could enlighten our conversation on the workings of religion is his understanding and theory of human nature. First of all, Kant categorically rejects Rousseau's theory that human beings are born morally good and become corrupted as they mutually influence or interact with each other in the social sphere. Second, he discards the Calvinist theology of original sin that human beings are intrinsically evil because they are born with a corrupted nature. The nature of religion is akin to the human nature. His understanding of human nature as intrinsically neither morally good nor morally evil also has significant consequences for his understanding of human history and progress. Kant seeks to walk a fine line. On the one hand, he is skeptical of the idea of moral progress whereby human beings can (and will) achieve human perfection. On the other hand, although human beings can never escape from the propensity to evil—a propensity—a propensity constitute of their species nature—there can be moral progress in history insofar as human beings can become actually good by virtue of their freedom. Kant's faith in (limited) moral and political progress is played out against a dark background, a realistic appraisal of "crooked humanity."[5]

Soyinka's critique of religious violence and terror orchestrated by religious fanatics and zealots is concomitant to his understanding of the human nature and the disposition of the will to make free spontaneous choices that could either ameliorate the human condition or exacerbate human life. In

1991, Wole Soyinka delivered the inaugural lecture in the Archbishop Olufosoye Lecture Series at the University of Ibadan entitled "The Credo of Being and Nothingness." In this seminal public address, Soyinka reflects theoretically and philosophically on the question of religion in both private and public sphere. He also discusses his personal attitude toward various religious worldviews and traditions. In the lecture, Soyinka informs his Nigerian audience that "the sphere of religion constitutes the ultimate challenge of the twenty-first century."[6] Commenting on the terrifying method religious imperialists and fanatics have used to transmit their faith, he announces that "It is not a new project; it dates back to the beginnings of man and has probably claimed more martyrs than most causes of human liberation. The dismal records of the Roman Catholic Inquisition are available to us, so is the iconoclasm of Protestant missionaries on African soil."[7]

For Soyinka, the sphere of religion is the sphere of violence. Violence is the underlying concept he employs to describe all religious activities and transactions in the modern world. He goes on to remark that "Violence appears to be the one constant in the histories of all the major religions of the world—a primitive aggressiveness, violence." The alternative to religious violence is radical humanism which promotes tolerance, peace, camaraderie, understanding, and ecumenical dialogue. While Soyinka stresses the practice and manifested presence of violence in the Abrahamic religions, their sacred texts often condemn and extol "holy hostility towards non-believers." Second to violence is the notion of intolerance and fear, which are produced deliberately by all religious fanatics, zealots, or extremists. As to the process of proselytization, Soyinka observes that religious zealots and radicals use the method of religious imperialism to win converts to their faith. These elements constitute the negative effects of religion in both political realm and civil society.

Most scholars and specialists of religion come to a similar conclusion that the history of religion and exchanges between various religious expressions in the modern world has been marked by enduring violence, reciprocal antagonism, and the extreme suffering of innocents. Critics of religion have also linked violence to power, greed, and the desire to dominate. For example, consider the following provocative titles highlighting the centrality of violence in religion: Karen Armstrong's Fields of Blood: Religion and the History of Violence (2014), and The Battle for God (2001), Russell Jacoby's Bloodlust: On the Roots of Violence from Cain and Abel to the Present (2014), Paul Copan's Is God a Moral Monster? Making Sense of the Old Testament God (2011), Mark Juergensmeyer's Terror in the Mind of God: The Global Rise of Religious Violence (2003), and Hent de Vries's Religion and Violence: Philosophical Perspectives from Kant to Derrida (2001). Among the represented authors include a religious scholar, historian, philosopher, public intellectual, theologian, and a political scientist; the shared intellectual interest among these thinkers is "the problem of how to reconcile evil with religious beliefs and convictions."[8] They're also apprehensive about the future of religion in the public life and oblige to reconsider the intricate relationship between religion and human responsibility in the modern world.

Most thinkers and experts on religion would agree that no existing religion promotes violence per se, but religious fundamentalists and imperialists use the instrumentalization of religion to enslave and colonize people and nations, inflict pain upon individuals, and disrupt the social order. Other critics have interpreted religion as a cultural production which highlights the systematic construction of truncated narratives designed to support avatars of religion and perpetuate structural inequities, structures of domination and subordination, forms of social oppression, and hegemonic transcendence.[9] Still for other thinkers, religions have fostered a narrative of injurious violence along with other bellicose and terrorist acts toward individuals throughout human existence. Mark Juergensmeyer, who has argued that religion is violent by nature, has written cogently about the obstinate and paradoxical nature of religion in human interactions:

> Within the histories of religious traditions—from biblical wars to crusading ventures and great acts of martyrdom—violence has lurked as a shadowy presence. It has colored religion's darker, more mysterious symbols. Images of death have never been far from the heart of religion's power to stir the imagination . . . Why does religion seem to need violence, and violence religion, and why is a divine mandate for destruction accepted with such certainty by some believers? Yet the forces that combine to produce religious violence are particular to each moment of history[10]

Radical atheist Christopher Hitchens once declared, "Religion had poisoned everything."[11] Interestingly, elsewhere, Hitchens retracts the statement that religion is not the most serious problem in the modern world but "Secular totalitarianism has actually provided us with the summa of human evil."[12] Yet, he qualifies his position by averring that

> For most of human history, the idea of the total or absolute state was intimately bound up with religion. A baron or king might compel you to pay taxes or serve in his army, and he would usually arrange go have priests on hand to remind you that this was your duty, but the truly frightening despotisms were those which also wanted the contents of your heart and your head . . . More than mere obedience was owed them: any criticism of them was profane by definition, and millions of people lived and died in pure fear of a ruler who could select you for a sacrifice, or condemn you to eternal punishment, on a whim.[13]

The summa of human evil should not be confined strictly to the realm of religion. As Berstein has brilliantly argued:

> There certainly has been a loss of the grip of traditional religious and theological discourse on people's every day lives. Traditionally, evil has been closely associated with religious, especially Christian, concerns. But today, there is a prevailing sense of the irrelevance of theodicy. If we think of theodicy in a broad sense as the attempt to find "justification" for the evil and useless suffering that we encounter, we might say, with Emmanuel Levinas, that we are now living in a time after "the end of theodicy." The philosophical problem . . . which is posed by the useless pain [mal] which appears in its fundamental malignancy across the events of the twentieth century concerns the meaning that religiosity and human morality of goodness can still retain after the end of theodicy.[14]

Richard Dawkins, in his influential and controversial text The God Delusion, seems to harmonize both Soyinka and Hitchens's dictum that religion is the source of evil in human history. He grounds the tragedy of the human condition and collective suffering in the world in the dark side of (religious claim of) absolutism. Consider his observation as expressed in this paragraph:

> It has to be admitted that absolutism is far from dead. Indeed, it rules the minds of a great number of people in the world today, most dangerously so in the Muslim world and in the incipient American theocracy. Such absolutism nearly always results from strong religious faith, and it constitutes a major reason for suggesting that religion can be a force for evil in the world.[15]

Soyinka associates religious violence with religious absolutism and dogmatism. Like many other humanists and critics of religion, he rightly understands religious absolutism and intolerance as a threat to cultural advancement, democratic peace, and human freedom and flourishing. He discerns that religious fanaticism in general presents a challenge to the security of human society and indeed its survival, and in the case of radical Islam in particular, it stirs global fear and extreme reactions cross-culturally.[16] In his impassionate book, Climate of Fear, presented first as a series of lectures for the prestigious Reith Lectures at Oxford University, Soyinka alarms his English audience that "We have to speak to religion!"[17] We ought to address the issue of religious indoctrination and the peril of religious radicalism and fanaticism. He continues, "We are obliged to recognize, indeed, to emphasize, the place of injustice, localized or global, as ready manure for the deadly shoots of fanaticism. However, the engines of global violence today are oiled from the deep wells of fanaticism, even though they may be cranked by the calculating hands of politicians or the power-hungry."[18]

Soyinka deploys the subject pronoun "we" to designate collective responsibility and mutual accountability in matters of religious peace and interfaith dialogue. Every member of society is somewhat liable to contribute to a non-threatening social order and an environment suitable to the absence of religious terror and violence. Without the collaborative effort of every individual, unrestrained religious expressions and precarious religious dogmas will continue to be a global crisis that haunts us. In other words, religion is something that needs to be controlled, and human evil premised on one's religious feeling and conviction heightens the human condition.

RELIGIOUS VIOLENCE AS A GLOBAL PREDICAMENT

Soyinka always links religious extremism with the pursuit of power and domination. Sam Harris observes that religious extremists "see political and military action to be intrinsic to the practice of their faith."[19] Religious fanatics and power-hunger politicians enjoy an inseparable alliance; more recently, "the poised blade of fanaticism has become more proficient and inventive over its agency of execution."[20] Lamentably, Soyinka declares, "the space of [religious] fanaticism aggressively expands into other nations of traditional tolerance and balance . . . The monologue, alas, continues to dominate the murderous swath blazed by succeeding religions—Christianity and Islam most notoriously. Deviationism—or heresy—is one shortcut to death."[21]

Furthermore, Soyinka resituates the ambivalent discourse of race to the zone of religion as the conundrum of the twenty-first century culture. Religion is now perceived as a global phenomenon of shock and human calamity. With dazzling rhetoric and linguistic force, he declares:

> The nineteenth-century black American scholar W.E.B. Du Bois once declared that the issue of the twentieth century would be that of race. It is becoming clear that while the century, the last, did indeed inherit—and still remains plagued almost continuously by—that social issue, race was replaced toward the end by religion, and it is something that has yet to be addressed with the same global concern as race once was. The issue of the twenty-first century is clearly that of religion, whose cynical manipulations contribute in no small measure to our current of fear.[22]

Soyinka goes on to clarify his thesis that religion not race is the predicament of the twenty-first century. He does that by first defining the integral components of religion and then by explaining the threatening implications of the program of religious fanaticism to cultures, peoples, and civilizations. What's at stake here is the dreadful and singular claim of religion: the call to absolute submission.

> Today, the main source of the fanatic mind is religion, and its temper—one that, ironically, is grounded in the doctrine of submission—has grown increasingly contemptuous of humanity, being characterized by arrogance, intolerance, and violence, almost as an unconscious vengeful recompense for its apprenticeship within the spiritual principle of submission.[23]

Religion, when it is imported by coercion or transmitted involuntarily, sustains "terror against terror, and the submission of the world to a regimen of fear."[24] To defend this thesis, Soyinka establishes the ambiguous rapport between religion, politics, and power: "To apprehend fully the neutrality of the power of fear in recent times, indifferent to either religious or ideological base, one need only compare the testimonies of Ethiopian victims under the atheistic order of Mengistu Mariam with those that emerged from the theocratic bastion of Iran under the purification orgy of her religious leaders. The Taliban remains a lacerating memory of antihumanism, as does the Stalinist terror in the former of Soviet Union."[25] Afterwards, he launches a warning:

> The axis of tension between power and freedom continues to propel the very motions of personality development, social upheaval, and nation conflicts. We must stress yet again that the urge to dominate may be the product of existing realities. Where such realities are not addressed, the political space is left fallow, enabling the calculating hand to fan the winds of fear . . . Power is self-sufficient, a replete possession, and must be maintained by whatever agency is required.[26]

In addition, he accentuates the intersection of faith, power, fear, and death:

> Power is, paradoxically, the primordial marshland of fear, from which emerges the precipitate of man's neurotic response to mortality. Therein he proceeds to attempt to match himself with the force of Nature, that agency through which the various apprehensions of God, Super Being, or whatever name—including Death—are filtered.[27]

The greatest threat to human freedom, peace, and harmony in the world is the scheme and politics of religious zealotry. Soyinka argues that religious extremism "menaces the peace of the world will make the uncomfortable discovery that this phenomenon is so much about religion, faith, or piety, but about power, domination, and its complementary idolization project unleashed on the rest of thinking humanity."[28] Religious zealots not only provoke horror but nurture an environment conducive to terror; as Soyinka maintains, "the assault on human dignity is one of the primary goals of fear, a prelude to the domination of the mind and triumph of power."[29] To put it another way, "the global climate of fear owes much to the devaluation or denial of dignity in the intersections of Communities, most notably between the stronger and weaker ones, an avoidance of the recognition of this very entitlement."[30]

Soyinka contemplates further on how Western religious imperialism and cultural imperialism had created violent societies and communities in Africa, as well led to social rift and disharmony among the African people. He sees both Christianity and Islam as agents of colonial conquest and violence in the Continent:

> Cultural and spiritual violation has left indelible imprints on the collective psyche and sense of identity of the peoples, a process that was ensured through savage repressions of cohering traditions by successive waves of colonizing hordes. Their presence was both physical and abstract. Their mission was not merely to implant their own peoples on any lands whose climates were congenial—East and Southern Africa—but to establish outposts for surrogate controls where the environment proved physically inclement . . . The cultural and spiritual savaging of the continent , let us hasten to insist, was not by the Christian-European axis alone. The Arab-Islamic dimension preceded it, and was every bit as devastating, a fact that a rather distorted sense of continental solidarity leads some scholars to edit, at the expense of Truth and reality. [31]

Both Christianity and Islam produced networks of power relations, hegemonic processes of dominance and oppression, and engineered the framework for cultural production of evil and religious resentment among the African people. The religious hegemony allowed both religious traditions "to secure the consent of subordinates to abide by their rule. The notion of consent is key, because hegemony is created through coercion that is gained by using the church, family, media, political parties, schools, unions, and other voluntary associations—the civil society and all its organizations." [32] In a complementary statement, Soyinka intensifies his thesis that "A new inhuman act, some new destructive conflict is certain to have surface somewhere, one that is traceable to one or other of the so-called major religions."[33]

On the other hand, Philosopher of religion Paul Copan has suggested we should think about other possibilities, and that religion has not poisoned everything. Let us attempt to find meaning in his provocative thought on the subject matter:

> Beyond this, history is littered with not-necessarily monotheistic tribes warring against each other or this communist government attacking that religious group. And why the focus on religion per se? Why not attack politics and political abuses of religion? What about ethnic tribalism that gives rise to hostility and violence, as in the former Yugoslavia? Why not consider complex sociological and historical factors that contribute to conflict? Alienation, poverty, disempowerment, racism/tribalism, power structures, historical feud-

ing, and animosity may rise to anger and then to violence. Religion often turns out to be the label used to justify violence between warring parties.

So why think that religion is the sole factor, the entire cause of blame? Rather than dragging God into the situation to cover over the root problem (s), we should resist the manipulation of God for our purposes. And what about the positive effects of a religion? What if more benefit than harm comes from a particular religion? The notion that religion causes violence or harm typically obscures a complexity of factors involved.[34]

THE CHALLENGE OF RELIGIOUS INTOLERANCE AND EXCLUSIVISM

Given the rampant spread of human violence and terror through the instrumentalization of dangerous religious convictions and daring ideologies, Soyinka calls for the obliteration of all religions in society. In an in an interview in 2002 with the South African journalist Peter Godwin, he declares unapologetically, "If religion was to be taken away from the world completely, including the one I grew up with, I'd be one of the happiest people in the world. My only fear is that maybe something more terrible would be invented to replace it, so we'd better just get along with what there is right now and keep it under control." Soyinka's call to "end" all public expressions deemed religious should be studied in its context and the history of religious violence in his own native land and in the modern world. Soyinka is not an anti-religion critic, but a fervent critic of religious terrorism and fanaticism.

In the same interview with Godwin, he declares, "I cannot imagine the religion I was brought up in having such complete contempt for human lives. And yet these are supposed to be the world religions. So that's why I consider myself rather fortunate that I've been able to see what other religions had to offer." Here, Soyinka is referring to a recent massacre in Federal Polytechnic College in the city of Mubi in northeastern Nigeria, in which 50 Nigerian students became victims of religious fundamentalism and violence. The Islamic religious militant group, known as Boko Haram, located in Northern Nigeria, orchestrated the crime in the first week of October in 2012. Initially, Boko Haram was linked with the al-Qaeda, and they collaboratively carried out a similar mission: the spreading of the Gospel of Islamic Jihadism, and devotion to Islam and the will of Allah.

Soyinka, having denounced the murderous orgy, argues that it is actually "the psychopaths of faith" who are guilty of bringing disrepute to the religion of Islam, whose mission, in the name of their prophet, constitutes the "commission of crimes that revolt our very humanity."[35] He deprecates his own country Nigeria for contributing to "international terrorism of the religious brand."[36] While he is unquestionably an enthusiast Nigerian Patriot, he is not a passive public intellectual and social critic.

Moreover, in an important statement, Soyinka exposes this baffling character of religious extremism: "Each major religion and even sect within the same religion appears periodically incapable of finding its own centre except by the act of reducing the other in some form or the other to nothing."[37] Although his target audience was Nigerian religious zealots, the moral of his provocation might be applicable cross-culturally and transnationally. Unquestionably, the human plague we call religious fanaticism has no boundary.

Religious intolerance has for its antecedence religious exclusivism, and is linked categorically to religious imperialism, which Soyinka construes as a menace to cultural relativism, democratic freedom, human rights, and religious diversity in the world. Soyinka coined the phrase "rhetorical hysteria" to theorize the perilous consequences of religion and to explain how religious exclusivists, extremists, and jihadists operate in the world. Let us provide a detailed description of the concept in order to establish rapport within the sphere of religion.

> Hysteria is not always an outwardly expressed abnormality, usually loud and violent. In fact, there is the quiet form of hysteria. Hysteria can also manifest itself as a collective and infectious outbreak, one that cannot always be accurately traced to a logical causative event. At its most affective, it emerges as the product of a one-way communication that succeeds in blinding its followers to the very realities that surround them while sealing them in a community of conviction, even of the unresolved kind. [38]

Rhetorical hysteria from a religious framework may be destructive, apocalyptic, disruptive, and contradictory "since it lays claim to rational processes yet acts with the dogmatism of pure revelation."[39] Soyinka contends that "Sadly, it is within the religious domain that the phenomenon of rhetorical hysteria takes its most devastating form."[40] What is susceptible about religious hysteria is that the thrust of its message is "embedded in an emotive fervent that may linger on, resulting in individual recalls, at various levels of consciousness, of the basic tenor of the collective experience, urging on the execution of its embedded message."[41] Agents of religious rhetorical hysteria promote a climate of mental fear in society. For example, Soyinka reiterates that radical Muslims or Islam extremism as practiced in Iran "has contributed, to a large extent, to the very condition of global intolerance, bigotry, and sectarian violence."[42] Comparatively, he exposes the same religious crisis in his own country, Nigeria:

> as suffered, in the intervening period, a spate of religion-motivated violence on an unprecedented scale, and is fast becoming only another volatile zone of distrust, unease, and tension . . . Our experiences in Nigeria—shared by numerous others—testify to the frequency of the lamentable conversion of the

mantra of piety to the promotion of the most hideous form of impiety, which, in my catechism, translates as the slaughter of other human beings in the cause of religious or any other conviction . . . It is an agonizing reversal to watch the faces of fanatics slavering after blood under the mandates of those same incantations.[43]

Consequently, Soyinka calls us to reason with him:

We have a duty to challenge a general reluctance to inquire why the adherents of some religions more than others turn the pages of their scriptures into a divine breath that fans the random homicidal spore to all corners of the world. Political correctness, itself an immobilizing form of hysteria, forbids the question, but, for those of us who prefer politically incorrect discourse to politically correct incineration or other forms of complicity in our premature demise, this question must be given voice.[44]

Atheist Humanist philosopher Daniel Dennett provides a profound thought on the bewildering message of religion to effectuate peace, tolerance, human dignity and solidarity in the world:

Indeed, many people think that the best hope for humankind is that they can bring together of the religions of the world in a mutually respectful conversation and ultimate agreement on how to treat one another. They may be right, but they don't know. The fervor of their belief is no substitute for good hard evidence, and the evidence in favor of this beautiful hope is hardly overwhelming. In fact, it is not persuasive at all, since just as many people, apparently, sincerely believe that world peace is less important, in both the short run and the long, than the global triumph of their particular religion over its competition. Some see religion as the best hope for peace, a lifeboat we dare not rock lest we overturn it and all of us perish, and others see religious self-identification as the main source of conflict and violence in the world, and believe just as fervently that religious conviction is a terrible substitute for calm, informed reasoning. Good intentions pave both roads.[45]

Nonetheless, the following questions that remain unanswered beg for further investigation:

Can religion peacefully cohabit with humanism in the twenty-first? In certain parts of the world the question indeed appears to be: Can religion cohabit with humanity itself? Such is the degree to which religion has either been central to, or has facilitated, the deadlines of conflicts, prodigally sacrificing humanity on alters erected even to mere differences in doctrinal niceties or historical interpretations, and most lethally when this occurs within the same faith.[46]

Despite the rhetorical tension in his language, and the shortcomings of his intellectual reasoning about religion, Soyinka is among the few theistic humanists who still maintain that the rmoral principles and religious values of the Yoruba religious cosmology may provide the best possible hope for humankind to deal with the problem of religious evil in the world, and to cultivate an ethic of tolerance, reciprocity, and a philosophy of relationality and human understanding. On the other hand, Bernstein has written perceptibly about the disposition of the will in regard to the freedom of choice:

> Ultimately, we cannot know why one person chooses to follow the moral law and another person does not. Nevertheless, from a practical point of view, we can (and must) postulate freely good or evil maxims. We are responsible for our individual choices and for overall moral character. Furthermore, this disposition is not something fixed and unchangeable a good person can become evil, and evil person can become good.[47]

In the subsequent chapter, we shall study Soyinka's interaction with African traditional religions and spirituality.

NOTES

1. Wiredu, *Cultural Universals and Particulars*, 46.
2. Qtd in Carnois, *The Coherence of Kant's Doctrine of Freedom*, 86.
3. Bernstein, *Radical Evil: A Philosophical Interrogation*, 13.
4. Cited in Berstein, *Radical Evil: A Philosophical Interrogation*, 23.
5. Bernstein, *Radical Evil: A Philosophical Interrogation*, 19–20.
6. Soyinka, *Art, Dialogue, and Outrage*, 239.
7. Ibid., 239–40.
8. Bernstein, *Radical Evil: A Philosophical Interrogation*, 2.
9. Townes, *Womanist Ethics and the Cultural Production of Evil*, 4, 19.
10. Juergensmeyer, *Terror in the Mind of God*, 6–7.
11. Hitchens, *God Is Not Great*, 27.
12. Ibid., 230.
13. Ibid., 230–1.
14. Bernstein, *Radical Evil: A Philosophical Interrogation*, 3.
15. Dawkins, *The God Delusion*, 286.
16. Soyinka, *Climate of Fear*, 26–7.
17. Ibid., 120.
18. Ibid.
19. Harris, *The End of Faith*, 110.
20. Soyinka, *Climate of Fear*, 122.
21. Ibid., 123.
22. Ibid., 124.
23. Ibid., 125.
24. Ibid., 28.
25. Ibid., 30–1.
26. Ibid., 48–51.
27. Ibid., 58.
28. Soyinka, *The Open Sore of a Continent*, 144.
29. Soyinka, *Climate of Fear*, 10.
30. Ibid., 100.
31. Soyinka, *The Burden of Memory, The Muse of Forgiveness*, 41–2.
32. Townes, *Womanist Ethics and the Cultural Production of Evil*. 20.
33. Soyinka, *Art, Dialogue, and Outrage*, 238.

34. Copan, *Is God a Moral Monster?* 200.
35. Soyinka, "*Psychopaths of Faith vs. The Muse of Irreverence,*" 13.
36. Soyinka, *Of Africa*, 188.
37. Ibid.
38. Soyinka, *Climate of Fear,* 63–4.
39. Ibid., 64.
40. Ibid., 85.
41. Ibid., 64.
42. Ibid., 83.
43. Ibid., 84–86.
44. Ibid., 87.
45. Dennett, *Breaking the Spell*, 16.
46. Soyinka, *Of Africa*, 136–7.
47. Bernstein, *Radical Evil,* 25.

Chapter Three

Soyinka's Interpretation of Ancestral Faith

Values and Meaning in African Traditional Religions

It is a common ideology that religion saturates every aspect of the African life. Generally, religious scholars have observed that the African people are very religious and spiritual. John Mbiti, an African religious scholar, has stated that "Africans are notoriously religious, and each people have its own religious system with a set of beliefs and practices. Religion permeates into all the departments of life so fully that it is not easy or possible always to isolate it."[1] E. Bolaji Idowu, writing about the religious world of the Yoruba (Soyinka's) people, has noted that "The real keynote of the life of the Yoruba is neither their noble ancestry nor in the past deeds of their heroes. The keynote of their life is their religion. In all things, they are religious. Religion forms the foundation and the all-governing principle of lifer for them ... The religion of the Yoruba permeates their lives so much that it expresses itself in multifarious ways."[2]

Consequently, it is possible to infer that religion serves as the social and humanistic source for the African moral vision and worldview, and the African humanistic values. This chapter establishes the values of African traditional religions and spirituality in the non-fictive works of Soyinka—as the subject relates to peace and harmony in the world. Soyinka argues that African traditional religions could be used as a catalyst to promote interreligious dialogue and understanding, and that they contribute to the preservation of life and promotion of shalom and human brotherhood in the world.

In his interpretation of African traditional religions—including the nature and attributes of African deities and the complexity of the Ifa in determining the divine will—Wole Soyinka presents African spirituality as a humanism in the same line of thought like Leopold Sedar Senghor, who, in his theorization of Negritude as "the sum total of the values of the civilization of the African World" (or "the sum of the cultural values of the black world"[3]) construes Negritude as a humanism of the twentieth century. What does Senghor mean by this concept? While Soyinka explains the concept through African spirituality and the concept of God in African religions, Senghor focuses on African concept of ontology and reality. Hence, we now turn to his thought on the subject matter:

> The paradox is only apparent when I say that negritude, by its ontology (that is, its philosophy of being), its moral law and its aesthetic, is a response to the modern humanism that European philosophers and scientists have been preparing since the end of the nineteenth century, and as Teilhard de Chardin and the writers and artists of the mid-twentieth century present it.
>
> Firstly, African ontology. Far back as one may go into his past, from the northern Sudanese to the southern Bantu, the African has always and everywhere presented a concept of the world which is diametrically opposed to the traditional philosophy of Europe. The latter is essentially *static, objective, dichotomic*; it is, in fact, dualistic, in that it makes an absolute distinction between body and soul, matter and spirit. It is founded on separation and opposition: on analysis and conflict. The African, on the other hand, conceives the world, beyond the diversity of its forms, as a fundamentally mobile, yet unique, reality that seeks synthesis . . .
>
> The African is, of course, sensitive to the external world, to the material aspect of beings and things. It is precisely because he is more so than the white Euroepan, because he is sensitive to the tangible qualities of things—shape, color, smell, weight, etc.—that the African considers these things merely as signs that have to be interpreted and transcended in order to reach the reality of human beings. Like others, more than others, he distinguishes the pebble from the plant, the plant from the animal, the animal from Man; but, once again, the accidents and appearances that differentiate these kingdoms only illustrate different aspects of the same reality. This reality is *being* in the ontological sense of the word, and it is life force. For the African, matter in the sense the Europeans understand it, is only a system of signs which translates the single reality of the universe: being, which is spirit, which is life force.[4]

This chapter suggests that the theoretical notions of radical theistic humanism and generous tolerance best summarize Soyinka's ideals and systems of thought on the matter of religious violence and intolerance. Unlike Western humanism that is antisupernaturalistic, African humanism is informed by religious metaphysics—the religious value and life of the African people. Soyinka's humanism is trapped within the religious ethos and sensibility and moral vision of the Yoruba people.

This chapter also contends that Soyinka presents African indigenous spirituality as a humanism for the twenty-first century, in the same manner

Leopold Senghor projected Negritude, which he defined as "the sum total of the values of the civilization of the African World," as a humanism of the twentieth century. Finally, the chapter and the next present Wole Soyinka as a religious critic and radical theistic humanist who affirms the contributions of African religions in the project of human solidary, open-mindedness, peace, and collaboration.

We shall now proceed with Soyinka's thought on the contribution of African religions in the discourse of world religions and the project of human solidary and tolerance. We begin by highlighting Soyinka's interpretation of God in African indigenous religions. In the process of our analysis, the connection with Senghor will become evident.

GOD IN AFRICAN RELIGION OR THE QUESTION OF GOD IN RELIGION

Furthermore, in the same lecture, Soyinka addresses the place of God in religion. God is perceived as a representative being in all theistic religions. Who is God? What are his attributes? How does he relate to the religions and human beings? What's the nature of God's relationship with the world? It is fundamental that all religions seek to answer these related questions. A second property of all religions is not simply the exaltation of God but also of truth and beauty which God fully embodies. In other words, theistic religions remind us consistently that "God is truth. God is truth; God is beauty."[5] Soyinka refutes the expected speculation that "wherever we find truth, wisdom, and beauty there also exists godhead."[6] If truth and beauty are universally acknowledged in all religions and among God's most distinctive attributes, Soyinka reasons, "can we not then simply agree among ourselves there wherever we find truth, then an element of godhead is present? That where there is beauty, and wisdom, there indeed exist aspects of godhead?"[7]

Soyinka answers his own rhetorical questions that "it will be sufficient to accept that wherever we find truth, wisdom and beauty in their purest essence, we have indeed glimpsed fundamental attributes of godhead."[8] Soyinka submits that all religions teach their adherents to imitate God by pursuing truth, wisdom, and beauty, which God himself signifies. Religion inculcates the aspiration in human beings "to approach, emulate or be worthy of godhead by assimilating and demonstrating these qualities in mundane activities, in social relationships and in the manifest creativity of the human mind. "[9] Therefore, Soyinka can conclude that "the ungodly in any religious conception are not therefore those who respond to the commonality of the intuition of godhead in a way different from ours, but those who set about the destruction of such manifestations whose idioms they do not understand."[10] From a critical realism perspective, Hicks has objected that "A critical religious realism affirms the transcendent divine reality which the theistic religions refer to as God, but is conscious that this reality is always thought and experienced by us in ways that are shaped and colored by human concepts and images."[11]

Soyinka subscribes to the belief that God is vital in theistic faiths, and religion is not religion without the appellation of the Divine. He writes with conviction that "Religion is built on the evocation of deities; a religion without a god, or the celebrated essence of one, is simply not a religion."[12] Most contemporary religious scholars would refute this claim, as it invalidates the religious category of non-theistic religions, and other signs or manifestations of religiosity that are anthropocentric (human-focus)—not theocentric (God-focus). Does religion need God? In his sociological study of religion, Emile Durkheim has brilliantly demonstrated that God is not a necessary element in religion.[13] Can man and woman live without God? Ravi Zacharias has intelligently articulated that God is a necessity in the human experience, and without him, life in this world is meaningless.[14] Finally, Paul Tillich has energetically argued that God as Being-Itself is the ground and power of all being.[15]

> The God of the theological theism is a being besides others and as such a part of the whole reality. He is certainly considered its most important part, but as a part and therefore as subjected to the structure of the whole. He is supposed to be beyond the ontological elements and categories which constitute reality. But every statement subjects him to them. He is seen as a self which has a world, as an ego which relates to a thought, as a cause which is separated from its effect, as having a definite space and endless time. He is a being, not being-itself. As such he is bound to the subject-object structure of reality, he is an object for us as subjects. At the same time we are objects for him as a subject.[16]

Tillich's dictum that God is the ground of all that exists has theological antecedent in African theological imagination about God. Orise "is the ancient name of God and not universally employed today among the Yoruba people, though it is commonly used among the Owo people (of Yorubaland) and among the Itsekiri and Western Ijaw."[17] Idowu's insightful commentary about African conception of God is quite relevant at this point:

> This name by derivation falls into two parts—*ori* and *se*. *Ori* is the essence of being and in the name of God it means "the very Source of Being" or "Source-Being." *Se* is a verb meaning "to originate." Thus the whole name means "the Source-Being which gives origin to all beings" or "the Source of all beings." This name occurs in various forms in several parts of Nigeria and in Dahomey. Among the Igbo we have a name which carries a similar or somewhat identical meaning and connotation. That is *Chukwu*. This is also falls into two parts— *Chi* and *Ukwu*. Chi is a very pregnant word. It carries the connotation of an overflowing fullness, the Main-Source or Main-Essence of Being. *Ukwu* means great, immense; it has also the connotation of a bundle of "that which

contains." *Chi-ukwu* thus means "the Immense, Overflowing Source of Being."[18]

Soyinka's most meaningful contribution to the question of God is unequivocally his accentuation on the suitability of the African deities or the Orisa of the Yoruba religion. Soyinka is cognizant about the deficiency of Western theology and religious curriculum. Few religious and divinity schools in the United States and West offer courses on African religions. If they do, Western teaching about God in African religion is often mischaracterized and misrepresented. For most Western scholars and scientists of religion, the African image of the divine does not matter because they have jettisoned African spirituality or the African experience in religion. The same manner they have categorically obliviated and deliberately erased Africa and Africans from the metanarratives of human history and universal civilizations, they have systematically excluded the African Gods in Western theological imagination. Consequently, Soyinka's goal was to include what has been omitted in scholarly discourse about religion and theology.

Moreover, Soyinka provides a brief overview of the nature and attributes of the African deities, their interaction with human beings, and their presence in the world. He avoids discussing the first order of theological significance such as the fall of man, sin, forgiveness, repentance, salvation, justification, the final judgment, etc.—such pertinent issues have great theological import in the Abrahamic religions. He has also failed to discuss how God and man/woman mutually respond to these concepts, and how these vital issues might potentially affect humanity's relationship with God. The absence of these "major problems" in Soyinka's religious writings might be warranted simply because they do not matter in African traditional religions; perhaps, Soyinka's own religious bias or ideology has preconditioned or hindered his interpretation of these theological matters.

In certain aspects, the African deities behave the same manner as the God of Judaism, Christianity, and Islam. In other aspects, such as described in the paragraph that follows, the African gods exhibit different attributes than those ascribed to the Judeo-Christian God. Generally, in African religions, "The real cohesive factor of religion is the living God and that without this one factor, all things would fall to pieces. Life belongs to God. It is he who summons it into being, strengthens and preserves it."[19] Soyinka comments with precision and clarity on the ontological transcendence and relational immanence of the African deities:

> In the process of their visitation, the gods assume form, shape, and character—and responsibilities. They acquire supervisory roles over phenomena, in some cases becoming thoroughly identified with them . . . the deities themselves appear to experience a need, periodically at least, to be united with the mortal essence, no matter the excuse—altruistic, self-sacrificial, in pursuit of moral

> redemption, or simply as an adventure in divine tourism . . . The gods are products of a primordial unity, as narrated in the myth of Atunda—literally rendered as "the one who recreates."[20]
>
> All gods, the Yoruba understand, are manifestations of universal phenomena of which humanity is also a part. Ife is replete with *odu*—those verses that form a compendium of morality tales, historic vignettes, and curative prescriptions—verses that narrate at the same time the experiences of both mortals and immortals for whom Ifa divined, counseled, and who either chose to obey or ignore Ifa. The skeptics are neither personalized nor hounded by any supernatural forces. The narratives indicative that they simply go their way . . . The gods remain totally indifferent toward who does or does not follow them or acknowledge their place in mortal decisions. The priest of Ifa never presumes to take up cudgels on behalf of the slighted deity. No excommunication is pronounced, a killing fatwa is unheard of. The language of apostasy is anathema in the land of the Orisa. There is neither paradise nor hell. There is no purgatory. You can neither seduce nor intimated a true Orisa faithful with projections of a punitive or rewarding afterlife . . . [21]

It seems to us the "secular African deities" also affirm various religious systems and traditions, and consider them "as equally legitimate religious alternatives, with preferences among them largely being functions of individual characteristics and social and cultural factors."[22] Next, Soyinka establishes the Orisa within their rightful place: the monotheistic religious tradition. He counters Hegel's famous claim that monotheism "represents the pinnacle of religious consciousness of which man is capable . . . [and that] a major deficit in the African's intelligence is his incapacity to conceive of a unified godhead."[23] Soyinka evaluates Hegel's reasoning about African religions and African intellectual faculty as a "baseless notion" and "sheer falsities" since:

> religions such as the Orisa actually acknowledge the existence of a supreme deity . . . There is absolutely no foundation in reason or logic that the ascending order of godhead in monotheistic form represents a higher development in man's conceptual capacities than the obverse. It is no more valid than an opinion that favors despotism above democracy.[24]

Many African theologians and religious scholars have claimed that pre-Christian monotheism existed in African concept of God and theological imagination. African theology "seeks the authenticity of continuity, first and foremost the continuity of God."[25] Andrew Lang in *The Making of Religion* posits that "Certain low savages are as monotheistic as some Christians. They have a Supreme Being, and the distinctive attributes of Deity are not by them assigned to other beings, further than as Christians assigns them to Angels, Saints, the Devil . . . "[26] E. Bolaji Idowu has claimed that "The Supreme Being of the primitive culture is a genuinely monotheistic Deity, described as Father, Creator, eternal, completely beneficent, ethically holy, and creatively omnipotent."[27] Accordingly, African spirituality belongs to the sphere of monotheism, and Africans are not polytheist, as traditionally depicted in Western imagination about the African religious experience.

Accordingly, African spirituality belongs to the world of monotheism, and Africans are not polytheists. Unlike, Regina Schwartz in *The Curse of Cain*, Soyinka does not subscribe to the thesis that the legacy of religious monotheism is violence, and that the belief in the unity of God allegedly leads to problems for everybody else." [28] As we will see in subsequent paragraphs, Soyinka accepts the maxim that "exclusive truth claims create an *us-them* mentality: to preserve *our* identity and religious purity, *they* must be removed."[29] He questions religious terrorism and imperialism as adequate method to force people to clinch to the "one true God." Let us reason about a possible inference: if "the absolutism of religion has been revealed especially in the notion of cosmic war,"[30] is it conceivable to prevent religious warfare in this age of religious violence and terrorism? Soyinka finds great promises in the tolerant and adaptive nature of African religions and the "secular gods" of the Yoruba people, which he proposes could potentially contribute to human peace and cooperation.

> What we must pursue, therefore, is not a competitive, bruising arena for the claims of ideology or religion but an open marketplace of both ideas and faiths. It is within this context, without any ambiguity, that the Orisa and their body of divine precepts, Ifa, prove of great humanistic value in the realm of religion. As quest, as the principle of spiritual enquiry, Ifa exemplifies this field of accommodation for all seekers, under no matter what structure of belief. This ancient religion that we have co-opted as a guide into our exploration of a noninterfering order of faith and spirituality proposes that "warfare between religions need not be. Its very nature protects it from the bellicose instinct that leads followers of other beliefs to defend even the most trivial annotation of their doctrinal text with their lives or, more accurately, with the lives of others, conveniently designated infidels, unbelievers, apostates, enemies of God, and other charitable epithets . . . Humanity is better served by the adoption of secularized deities than by those other gods of undoubtedly entrancing liturgies that evoked as control zones on humanity, tyrannized over by morals, no different from ourselves.[31]

On one hand, Soyinka would have us to believe that religion in general is the source of human suffering and violence in human history. On the other hand, he presents the Yoruba religious tradition as a possible solution to the human predicament and the problem of religious tolerance in the modern world. Africa seems to prioritize the value of one religion over another, chiefly African traditional religions. This particular stance could be seen as an ambiguous attitude of Soyinka toward all faiths. Consider this important paragraph that reveals the democratic and tolerant nature of the Orisa:

> Religion, or profession of faith, cannot serve as the common ground for human coexistence except of course by the adoption of coercion as a principle and, thus, the manifestation of its corollary—hypocrisy—an outward conformism that is dictated by fear, by a desire for preferment, or indeed, the need for physical survival. In the end, the product is conflict, and the destruction of cultures. Let this be understood by the champions of theocracies where religion and ideology meet and embrace. Orisa admonishes them: you will not bring the world even close to the edge of combustion. The essence of Orisa is the antithesis of tyranny, bigotry, and dictatorship—what greater gift than this respect, this spirit of accommodation, can humanity demand from the world of the spirit?
>
> Thus, for all seekers after the peace and security of true community, and the space of serenity that enables the quest after truth, pleading for understanding from the Orisa for this transgression of their timeless scorn of proselytizing, we urge yet again the simple path that travelled from the soil of the Yoruba across the African landmass to continuous nations, across the hostile oceans to the edge of the world in the Americas—*Go to the Orisa, learn from the Orisa, and be wise.*[32]

Admittedly, Soyinka is proselytizing individuals to the Yoruba faith and spirituality. It also appears that he is expressing a particular brand of religious exceptionalism—a thesis he will refute—committing the similar transgression of the Christians and Muslims, whom he fiercely opposes? Perhaps, Soyinka is unable to reconcile intellectually this internal tension and rhetorical ambiguity—within himself. Is he being impartial? Is he demonstrating religious favoritism?

Because of the openness and fluidity of African religions, Soyinka strongly believes that they could be used potentially as agents of social transformation to the dilemma of religious exclusivism and religious violence in the world.

> For the rest, I wish only to exhort you: study the spirituality of this continent. As in all things, selectiveness is the key. To limit myself to that with which I am on familiar grounds, I say to you: go to the *orisa*, learn from them and be wise. The religion of the *orisa* does not permit, in tenets, liturgy, catechism or practice, that pernicious dictum: "I believe, therefore I am." Nowhere will you find the sheerest skein of reasoning in that direction to human self-apprehension. Obviously, therefore, you will not find its corollary: "You do not believe, therefore you are not." *Orunmila* does not permit it. *Obatala* cannot conceive of it. Ogun will take up arms against it. No one *odu* of IFA so much as suggests it. It is not weakness in the character of this religion however, it is not even tolerance. It is simply—understanding. Wisdom. An intuitive grasp of the complexity of the human mind, and a true sense of the infinite potential of the universe.[33]

At this point, we shall turn our attention briefly to Senghor's thought about God in order to show further points of convergence and confluence between his ideas and those of Soyinka. Senghor's instructive explanation about the African concept of God will help fill the intellectual gap:

> The whole universe appears as an infinitely small, and at the same time an infinitely large, network of life forces which emanate from God and end in God, who is the source of all life force. It is He who vitalizes and devitalizes all other beings, all the other life forces . . . It is by bringing the complementary life force together in this way that Man reinforces them in their movement towards God and, in reinforcing them, he reinforces himself; that is, he passes from *existing to being*. He cannot reach the highest form of being, for in fact only God has this quality; and He has it all the more fully as creation, and all that exists, fulfill themselves and express themselves in Him . . . We have seen what constitutes for the African the "deep resemblance between Man and the world." For him, then, the act of restoring the order of the world by re-creating it through art is the reinforcement of the life forces in the universe, and consequently, of God, the source of all life forces—or, in other words, the Being of the universe. In this way, we reinforce ourselves at the same time, both as interdependent forces and as beings whose being consists in revitalizing ourselves in the re-creation of art.[34]

Leaving the conversation on monotheism aside for a moment, Soyinka pursues another facet of the religious experience: the difference between religion and cults. Let us consider his first observation:

> Nearly every religion develops sects, even cults, which then proceed to act contrary to the fundamental precepts and articles of faith that religion. It is said that many of those who comment on African religions are ignorant of the differences between religions and cults in general on the one hand, and between religion and those specific cults which spring up in relation to certain observances within that religion.[35]

He goes on to opine that a deity is essential for religion, whereas in cults, it is not a requirement. However, he accepts the idea that "cults may attach to religion in order to harvest a ready membership and ride on spiritual intensity."[36] The phenomenon of cultism in West Africa demands our particular attention. Soyinka associates certain African cults such as the historic *Iya* in former Dahomey—now Republic of Benin—and the *Gelede* of Western Nigeria—with power, wealth, political influence, and terrorism. He notes that they were used "as power devices that operated through secret rituals, oath-taking, and thus, fear of the vengeance of malevolent forces for apostates and oath-breakers, if anything, purely political instruments of power and terror. They were used to acquire wealth, consolidate political positions, and keep other sections of the community in their place."[37]

Soyinka advances the conversation forward by revealing the dark side of religious cults when he writes "Cults are mostly secretive instruments of power, even where they can be proved to have sprung from the genuine religion."³⁸ Soyinka's reflections on these various religious expressions should not be regarded as new information in the scientific study of religion; Soyinka's new contribution to the conversation, however, is brilliant defense of the viability of African traditional religions and their inclusion among world's great religions.

Briefly, we suggest ten theological truths that all three Abrahamic religions (i.e. Judaism, Christianity, and Islam) and African traditional religions confess about God:

1. Jews, Christians, Muslims, and adherents to African traditional religions believe in the unity (oneness) of God and that there is only one God (both Jewish and Christian theologians call that the doctrine of monotheism or "tawhid" in Islamic theology).
2. Jews, Christians, Muslims, and adherents to African traditional religions believe that God is transcendent and uncreated (that is, God has always existed; he has no beginning and no end. Theologians use the theoretical concept "aseity" to describe this phenomenon about God)
3. Jews, Christians, Muslims, and adherents to African traditional religions believe God is Creator of everything and Sovereign Lord of the universe.
4. Jews, Christians, Muslims, and adherents to African traditional religions believe that God's knowledge of the present, past, and future is comprehensive and exhaustive.
5. Jews, Christians, Muslims, and adherents to African traditional religions believe that God created the first human beings: Adam and Eve.
6. Jews, Christians, Muslims, and adherents to African traditional religions believe that God created human beings to serve, worship, and honor Him.
7. Jews, Christians, Muslims, and adherents to African traditional religions believe that God is love, just, and compassionate.
8. Jews, Christians, Muslims, and adherents to African traditional religions believe that God cannot be known by human beings; rather, God himself has revealed Himself to humanity—through chosen individuals known as prophets.
9. Jews, Christians, Muslims, and adherents to African traditional religions believe that God has also revealed Himself through a Book; Jews call this sacred text the Hebrew Bible/Scriptures (Old Testament); Christians call it the Bible—which includes both the Old Testament and New Testament—and Muslims call their book the Qur'aran. African traditional religions do not have or claim a Sacred Text.
10. Jews, Christians, Muslims, and adherents to African traditional religions has reserved a judgement day in which he will judge all people, punish all evildoers, and rewards everyone according to his/her deeds.

There are also great theological divides and differences between Jews, Christians, and Muslims about the same God they confess. For example, Christians believe God exists in three Persons: God the Father, God the Son, and God the Holy Spirit. Christian theologians call this special aspect about God the trinity. Both Muslims and (orthodox) Jews reject the doctrine of the trinity. Orthodox Jews are still waiting for God to send the Jewish Messiah; Christians believe that Jesus is/was the Jewish Messiah promised by God in the Hebrew Bible (Old Testament); and Muslims do not believe that Jesus is/was the Jewish Messiah.

Further, Christians confess the full deity and humanity of Jesus; that is Jesus is God, and that God incarnated in the historical person named Jesus. Christians also believe that Jesus is the final revelation of God and that no one can come through God except through Jesus (that is Jesus is the only way to God). Both orthodox Jews and Muslims reject the finality and supremacy of Jesus. Muslims believe Mohammed, not Jesus, is the final revelation of God.

THE SACRIFICE OF AFRICA

In our previous analysis, we have examined Soyinka's thought and attitude toward religious violence and his criticism of spiritual dogmatism, and the concept of God in African traditional religions. While he denounces the violence spread by Christian and Islamist extremists, Soyinka celebrates the irenic nature of African traditional religions. He maintains that the indigenous faiths of Africa do not promote deadly fanaticism and religious imperialism. He also claims that African religions stimulate open-mindedness and contagious tolerance to other faiths. Yet, he laments that African religions are "those 'invisible religions' that the world continues to ignore as possible sources of cultural arbitration."[39] For the detractors of Africa, "Africa does not exist, much less matter."[40] In an apologetic tone, he writes constructively and meritoriously about the vitality of African indigenous spirituality and its contribution to the campaign for world peace and human solidarity:

> The spirituality of the black continent in the religion of the *orisa,* abhors such principles of coercion or exclusion, and recognizes all manifestations of spiritual urgings as attributes of the complex disposition of godhead. *Tolerance* is synonymous with the spirituality of the black continent, *intolerance* is anathema![41]

Unlike the Abrahamic religions, African religions don't seek to convert or proselytize atheists, (non-theistic) humanists, or non-believers, nor has historically engaged in vehement conquest to gain territory jurisdiction or hegemonic domination:

> African religions do not proselytize, but let me break with that tradition yet again in the worthy cause of a global quest for harmonized coexistence, and offer the world a lesson from African spirituality, taken specifically from the religion of the Orisa, the pantheon of faith of the Yoruba people. This religion, one that is still pursued in Brazil and others parts of South America and the Caribbean, has ever engaged in any equivalent of the crusade or the jihad in its own cause. The words *infidel, unbeliever, kafiri* are anathema to its scriptures; thus it does not recognize a spiritual division of the world.[42]

Soyinka advances this conversation by underscoring the exceptional character of African religions in the preservation of African cultural identity and practices. African spirituality is a form of resistance to foreign oppression:

> Religions do exist, such as on this continent, that can boast of never having launched a war, any form of jihad or crusade, for the furtherance of their beliefs. Yet those beliefs have proved themselves bedrocks of endurance and survival, informing communities as far away as the Caribbean and the Americas . . . The religions of this continent rescued us as conscious race in the Diaspora, preserved our identity and, what is more, infected even those claimants to a superior knowledge of the Supreme Deity—those religions whose exalted high priests sometimes claim to be on first-name acquaintance with their deities, on whose personal authority they mete out diabolical punishments to unbelievers, even for secular activities.[43]

Soyinka celebrates the legacy of African religions for their leniency and flexibility toward alien religious expressions. African religions empowered enslaved Africans to endure slavery, white oppression and violence, and ultimately, they served as catalyst for collective emancipation in North America, Latin America, and the Caribbean isles. The virtue of African spirituality is the fact that it is incompatible with human oppression.

> Despite its reticence, however, it has penetrated the globe and survived in the confident retention by the displaced and dispossessed slaves, its infections hold extending even to their European violators. Its watchword is tolerance, a belief that there are many paths to truth and godhead, and that the world should not be set on fire to prove the supremacy of a belief or the righteousness of a cause.[44]
>
> Unfortunately, African religions have been marginalized by the aggressive, often bloody intrusion of Christianity and Islam onto this continent, a spirituality which, despite its seeming effacement, has continued to spread across the globe, providing sources of spiritual strength to our kin in the Diaspora and acting as a rallying-point in their struggle for liberation and human dignity . . . Their validity remains unchanged and they repeat a necessary warning against the unrepentant in this stubborn reiteration of the Nothingness credo against African spirituality.[45]

Furthermore, in his postcolonial critique of Islam and Christianity, Soyinka provocatively denounces both traditions for inflicting tremendous pain on the African people and radically altered their culture and tradition.

> Both Islam and Christianity have been guilty not merely of physical atrocities on African soil, including enslavement of the indigenes, but of a systematic assault on African spirituality in their contest for religious hegemony. Therefore the claims of either religion to mutual tolerance, I proposed, were still limited to the binary insularity of the world's incorrigible hegemonists, since they have proved incapable of taking into consideration the rights of other religions to equal respect, equal space, and tolerance.[46]

On the cultural and religious level, V. Y. Mudimbe describes the process by which Western colonial missionaries pugnaciously partitioned and changed African societies:

> The new *espace metisse* was allowed by at least three factors that made a complete reproduction of the Western model difficult. First, the reformation of the indigenous past in what is signified as violence for rewriting a genesis created a spirit of resistance among the indigenous people. In order to protect their memory, they moved their most signifying practices from an open to a hidden social space, often restructuring in newly organized esoteric lines what were before the popular narratives and rituals of the colonial experience . . . Second, another factor that made a complete conversion problematic: the barrier of languages. Colonial policies encouraged missionaries to describe indigenous languages in a systematic manner and, generally, promoted their work for standardizing certain idioms. Nevertheless, the existing multitudes of languages reflected itself as a barrier for the penetration of both the colonial rationality and the Christian message . . . Briefly, in the socioeconomic and cultural reconfiguration of Africa in the nineteenth and early twentieth centuries; an *espace metisse* imposes itself against the far from peaceful ancient traditions and the newly substituted program in colonial history. No wonder that the consciousness produced by this new space sometimes questions the validity of what is affirmed as truth, and beneath the confluence of currents that made it possible . . . that accounts for the power of the Western will to truth.[47]

Soyinka also reveals that, in seeking to implant a corrective spirituality, both Christianity and Islam have effected cultural alienation and human aggression and conflict in the Continent. They were bonded together to obscure the indigenous beliefs and spiritual practices, and altered organic relationships between man and environment.[48] He decries the violent conquest of Islam and Christianity and laments over the cultural destruction orchestrated by external forces and influences:

> Both religions came and subverted the organic systems of belief that preexisted their arrival, religions older and, in many aspects, more humane than the manifested tenets of their own. The Euro-Christian armies of conquest, fast on the heels of missionaries and early adventurers, plundered and looted African civilizations, burnt and smashed priceless carvings, which, from the point of view, were nothing but manifestations of idolatry and satanism. Conversion to Christianity was, admittedly, sometimes by persuasion, more often it was enforced—through military conquest, terror of enslavement, and punitive (economic) controls.[49]

As a result, he calls for the complete eradication of all foreign religious practices and expressions in Africa: "I have stated my preference: Let us expel alien religions altogether in all forms."[50] This proclamation seems to be conflicting with Soyinka's liberal openness to other religious traditions and his embrace of religious inclusivism and tolerance. Soyinka does not question the religious syncretism that is prevalent in the continent nor does he find it problematic. Jacob Olupona's informative and insightful observation about the dynamics of Islam and Christianity in African societies will shed further light on the issue:

> Africa domesticated the two exogenous religions. While Islam and Christianity both came to African from outside, both traditions have been present on the African continent for nearly as they have existed. This means that Africans have had centuries to develop unique adaptations to Christian and Islamic practices, and theologies to make them well suited to African needs. It also means that in many respects neither to be considered particularly foreign to Africa; in some cases, their African forms are older than certain "traditional religions." In the same way that Islam and Christianity have changed, so too have traditional religions, which in some cases have adopted entirely new forms. This is an important corrective to the tendency to view traditional religions as old and global religions as new. In fact, all religions are always changing and incorporate new aspects into their practices.[51]

Lannin Sanneh also comments intelligently on the religious encounters and the interpenetration of these faiths:

> In the African situation, we find Muslims adopting elements from the local religions and blending these with their practice of Islam—as in fact happened—then it is clear that the Islamic code as it exists in the law books has been displaced as a determinant of religious perception . . . In the encounter with traditional religions, African Muslims have delineated the situation in terms of what Islam permits (halal) and what it forbids (haram). In this way judgment is made on the methods and forms of traditional religious worship and divination, not on the content and ideas. Ifa divination, for example, is assessed on the basis of whether it contravenes the religious code, not on whether it introduces people to ideas of the supernatural. African Christians, on the other hand, would seem to be attracted to those features of Ifa which

prepared people for faith in the Creator and His Providence, considering as of less consequence thee forms and methods of Ifa practice. It is this religious culture of African religions which acquired a new importance in the Christian setting.[52]

Soyinka has not addressed the issue of "interreligious transformation" as African indigenous religions encountered the influence of Islam and Christianity. In fact, he praises African religions for being accommodative to alien faiths, which could be viewed both as a positive and negative affect:

> Yoruba society is full of individuals, who worship the Anglican God on Sundays, Sacrifice to Sango every feastday, consult *Ifa* before any new project and dance with the Cherubim and Seraphims every evening . . . No spiritual conflict is created within them and no guilt is experienced. Being unwesternised in religious attitudes, that is, not slavishly tried to the western concept of a single form of worship for the attainment of spiritual exaltation or divine protection, they live without any internal contradictions.[53]

At this juncture, Soyinka's point of view on the interplays and approachability of African religions does not contract his praise report about African indigenous spirituality, and his claim that they possess inherent value and wisdom to potentially cure the conundrum of religious bigotry and zealotry in the modern world. On the contrary, when a foreign religion is grafted in the receiving ("occupied") religion, it is conceivable that the imported faith would alter the nature and constitutive elements of the receiving religion; thus, it will become a "fragmented religion." Secondly, both African Islam and African Christianity do not work well with the indigenous faiths. The interreligious conflict is inevitable, almost necessary.

Next, Soyinka sees Christianity as a slave religion, and condemns Western Christianity for supporting the selling of African flesh to European slavers: "A religion that separated humanity into the saved and the damned—the latter being qualified for mass deportation to distant lands as beasts of burden—can hardly be considered fundamentally compatible with the people on whom such a choice was imposed . . . From the West coast of Africa to southern Africa, the story is the same."

In the same line of thought, Soyinka posits that the Arab-Islamic record in Africa was not an improvement. He is in an agreement with George Hardy, the author of *l'Art negre* (1927), that "Islam began the work of destruction"[54] in the continent. The crime of Islam is comparable to that of colonial Christianity, Soyinka maintains.

> Conversions for the glory of an equally alien deity. Nothing that the Islamic invaders encountered was sacred; all was profane except the sword and the book of Allah. They set the precedent for compelling converts to shed their indigenous names, names that narrated their beginnings and conferred on them

their individual and historic identities. They inaugurated the era of slave raids on the black continent for Arab slave markets. The routes of slave caravans began from the central and eastern heartlands of the continent, stretched through Northern Africa to Saudi Arabia, or passed over the waters by slave dhows from Madagascar and *Dar es Salaam* to Yemen, Omar, etc.[55]

Soyinka's condemnation of Jihadist Christianity and Islam is vindicated on historical record. He is indignant about the method (religious imperialism, terror, and fear) the colonizers used to introduce the natives to their religion and spread their faith across the Continent: "Africa was enslaved under the divine authority of the Islamic Christian gods, their earthly plenipotentiaries, and commercial stormtroopers."[56] What is then the burden and hope of reconciliation as the title of Soyinka's book (*The Burden of Memory, The Muse of Forgiveness*) indicates? How should Africans now respond to these historic atrocities and violence inspired by religion in the postcolonial moment?

While Soyinka is not attempting to malign the memory of the African past or dismiss the grievous affects and consequences of religious violence on the Continent and its people, he nevertheless finds a way to talk honestly about both conflict and healing; the memory of religious viciousness of the (African) past caries over an inexorable weight of shame and dishonor on the (African) present:

> Every landmark is a testament of history, and in our own indelible instance—from Goree through the slave forts of Ghana to Zanzibar—every fort and stockade, increasingly turned into museums, is filled with grim evocations of this passage of our history. They are indices of Truth, an essence and a reality that offer any peoples, however impoverished, a value in itself, a value that, especially when rooted in anguish and sacrifice, may dictate a resolve for redemption and strategies for social regeneration. To act in any way that denigrates the lessons, the imperatives of that Truth, for demagogic or other opportunistic reasons, is to pollute a people's Source, and declare a new round of exterior control of a people's heritage.[57]

Soyinka is critical about the value of Christianity or Islam to foster peace and camaraderie in the modern world. He is persuaded that the world should turn to African spirituality and traditional religions to learn meaningful life lessons about tolerance, human dignity, interdependence, and mutual reciprocity; as he declares, "Today, there is urgent need for Mother Religion, of whatever inclination, to come to the rescue of humanity with the benevolent of infanticide."[58] As we have discussed in preceding pages, in his book *Of Africa*, Soyinka once again highlights the place of African spirituality in promoting peace, freedom, and humanistic values. He establishes close relationship between African indigenous religions and the creed of humanism. We shall expand further on Soyinka's humanism and his call for religious tolerance in the final chapter.

NOTES

1. Mbiti, *African Religions & Philosophy*, 1.
2. Idowu, *Olddumare—God in Yoruba Belief*, 5.
3. Senghor, "Negritude: Humanism of the Twentieth Century," in Olaniyan and Quayson (eds), *African Literature*, 196.
4. Senghor, "Negritude: Humanism of the Twentieth Century," 197–8.
5. Soyinka, *Art, Dialogue, and Outrage*, 240.
6. Ibid., 240–41.
7. Ibid., 240.
8. Ibid.241.
9. Ibid.
10. Ibid.
11. Hick, "Religious Realism and Non-Realism: Defining the Issue," in Trigg, *Religious Diversity: Philosophical and Political Dimensions*, 47.
12. Soyinka, *Of Africa*, 145.
13. Durkheim, *The Elementary Forms of the Religious Life* (1912)
14. Zacharias, *Can Man Live Without God?* (2004)
15. Tillich, *Systematic Theology* (1957).
16. Tillich, *The Essential Tillich*, 189.
17. Idowu, "God," In Dickson and Ellingworth, *Biblical Revelation and African Beliefs*, 25.
18. Idowu, "God," 25.
19. Idowu, *African Traditional Religion*, 104.
20. Soyinka, *Of Africa*, 158.
21. Ibid., 147–8, 150–1.
22. Netland, *Encountering Religious Pluralism*, 221.
23. Soyinka, *Of Africa*, 131.
24. Ibid.
25. Lawrie, Christianity and the African Imagination, 9.
26. Lang, The Making of Religion, 180.
27. Idowu, "God," 18.
28. Qtd in Copan, *Is God a Moral Monster?* 198. The statement is originated from Regina Schwartz.
29. Ibid.
30. Juergensmeyer, *Terror in the Mind of God*, 220.
31. Soyinka, *Of Africa*, 134–5.
32. Ibid., 168.
33. Soyinka, *Art, Dialogue, and Outrage*, 246.
34. Senghor, "Negritude: Humanism of the Twentieth Century," 198, 199, 202.
35. Soyinka, *Art, Dialogue, and Outrage*, 242.
36. Soyinka, *Of Africa*, 145.
37. Ibid.
38. Ibid., 130.
39. Soyinka, *Of Africa*, 193.
40. Ibid., 194.
41. Soyinka, *The Burden of Memory, The Muse of Forgiveness*, 48.
42. Soyinka, *Climate of Fear*, 136.
43. Soyinka, *Art, Dialogue, and Outrage*, 239.
44. Soyinka, *Climate of Fear*, 136.
45. Soyinka, *Art, Dialogue, and Outrage*, 239.
46. Soyinka, *Of Africa*, xi-xii.
47. Mudimbe, *Tales of Faith*, 152–4.
48. Soyinka, *The Burden of Memory, The Muse of Forgiveness*, 49–52.
49. Ibid., 52.
50. Soyinka, *Art, Dialogue, and Outrage*, 302.
51. Olupona, *African Religions: A Very Short Introduction*, 89.

52. Sanneh, *West African Christianity: The Religious Impact*, 227–8, 236.
53. Soyinka, *Art, Dialogue, and Outrage*, 302.
54. Soyinka, *The Burden of Memory, The Muse of Forgiveness*, 52.
55. Ibid., 53.
56. Ibid.
57. Soyinka, *The Burden of Memory, The Muse of Forgiveness*, 59–60.
58. Soyinka, *Climate of Fear*, 121.

Chapter Four

In Praise of Shalom and Human Solidarity

The Logic of Radical Humanism, and The Value of Generous Tolerance

It is indisputable that Wole Soyinka is a champion of humanist values and religious inclusivism. Soyinka has modelled an exemplary life of public intellectualism and literary ingenuity, through which he promotes humanism as a worldview, and African spirituality as an alternative to the Abrahamic religions. In regard to this matter, we suggest that the theoretical notions of radical theistic humanism and generous tolerance best summarize Soyinka's ideals and systems of thought. The subsequent paragraphs outline several characteristics of Soyinka's humanism and situate him within the African humanism and African religious traditions. Soyinka's humanism is trapped within the religious ethos and sensibility, and moral vision of the Yoruba people. In his quest for relevance, Soyinka presents African theistic humanism and indigenous spirituality, in the words of the eminent Kenyan novelist and literary critic Ngũgĩ wa Thiong'o, "as a liberating perspective within which to see ourselves clearly in relationship to ourselves and to other selves in the universe."[1]

The radicalism of Soyinka's humanism is warranted because of its strong religious resonance—unlike most modern humanists who categorically reject theism as an option. Soyinka rejects the non-theistic Western humanism to embrace a different brand of humanism sourced in African traditional theistic humanism and African culture and thought. That does not mean he was not also influenced by western humanism. Soyinka's generous tolerance is grounded in the personality of the Yoruba deities and the tractability of

African traditional religions. As we have shown in our analysis, African religions are generous to accommodate alien faiths and are subject to contingencies. Soyinka's humanism is a creative intellectual and spiritual enterprise that does not split the life of the mind and the life of faith. The promotion of human welfare is the basis of its foundation. William R. Jones has insightfully commented on the workings of humanism:

> Religious humanism exists as a philosophical/theological *perspective* and not as an on-going *institution* . . . Because humanism affirms radical freedom/ autonomy as the essence of human reality, humanism is most prominent in those cultures where individuals exercise in fact considerable control over their environment and history. The humanist understanding of wo/man comes into being, it appears, as the consequence of this type of experience and the material situation it presupposes.[2]

Prominent Ghanian Kwama Gyekye has shrewdly remarked:

> The humanist norms of traditional African society most probably were at the base of the interpretations of the communitarian system as a form of socialism. That the traditional morality of African societies was preoccupied with human welfare has been noted in some studies. If one were to look for a pervasive and fundamental concept in African socioethical thought generally—a concept that animates other intellectual activities and forms of behavior, including religious behavior, and provides continuity, resilience, nourishment, and meaning to life—that concept would most probably be humanism: a philosophy that sees human needs, interests, and dignity as of fundamental importance and concern. For, the art, actions, thought, and institutions of the African people, at least in the traditional setting, reverberate with expressions of concern for human welfare . . . The humanist and social strand of the African socioethical thought and life is reflected in the African perception of the place of religion in human life.[3]

Unlike Western humanism, African indigenous humanism is not anti-supernaturalistic or anti-religious. African indigenous humanism maintains a rigid supernaturalistic metaphysics that is rejected by Western nontheistic humanism.[4] Lewis Gordon has stated that "If we define humanism as a value system that places priority on the welfare, worth, and dignity of human beings, its presence in precolonial African religious and philosophical thought can easily be found."[5] From the perspective of the Akan humanism in Ghana, Kwame Gyekye offers an informative commentary on the matter:

> The position of Akan thinkers here is quite different. In their view, the pursuit of the welfare and interest of human beings in this world—which for them, as for every humanist, is the crucial meaning of humanism—need not lead to the rejection of supernaturalism. It is possible, they maintain, to believe in the existence of supernatural entities without necessarily allowing this to detract

from the pursuit of human welfare in this world . . . In Akan thought this tension between supernaturalism and humanism does not appear; for the Akan, religion is not seen as hindering the pursuit of one's interests in this world. on the contrary, the supernaturalistic outlook of Akan humanism is the consequence not only of a belief in the existence of a Supreme Being and other supernatural entities, but, more importantly I think, of a desire to utilize the multificence and powers of such entities for the promotion of human welfare and happiness.[6]

The fundamental thrust of Soyinka's radical humanism is the elevation of human dignity, needs, and interests, and the pursuing of the common good. As he asserts, dignity "captures the essence of self-worth, the sheer integrity of being that animates the human spirit, and the ascription of equal membership in the human community."[7] Soyinka's humanism lies in the bundles of human virtues: "integrity, love, tenderness, graciousness, generosity, or indeed the spirit of self-sacrifice. Dignity, however, appears to give the most accessible meaning to human self-regarding."[8] Elsewhere, he reminds us that "dignity in the management of Community lies at the heart of our preoccupation . . . Dignity is simply another face of freedom, and thus the observe of power and domination, that axis of human relationship that is equally sustained by fear—its poles doomed to remain permanent conflict, yet complement each other."[9] Hegemony is the ethos of religion driven by fear and terror. Such attitude transgresses the values of theistic humanism.

At the World Humanist Congress held in 2014, Wole Soyinka was honored with the International Humanist Award from The British Humanist Association. In presenting the award to Soyinka, the trustee, Patricia Rogers, defended the organization's choice in this statement: "In the sharpest possible contrast to the terrorist Boko Haram's dichotomous disavowal of 'western education' as alien to their world, Soyinka has long been the intellectual leader of distinctively African voices within the universal Enlightenment tradition." Because of illness, Soyinka was unable to attend the ceremony; therefore, he accepted the award via a recorded audio. It is to the text of the recording we now turn to explore Soyinka's form of humanism.

It is good to inform the readers that the message of Soyinka's acceptance speech should be understood within the cultural backdrop and historical violence of the Nigerian Islamist extremist group known as Boko Haram. In April 2014, the religious extremists of Boko Haram adducted 276 schools girls from a learning center in Chibok, Borno. Hence, we can anticipate Soyinka to denounce the crime in his speech.

Generally, Soyinka's radical humanism is against any form of human terror and oppression. Its basic goal is the betterment of humanity and the elevation of human dignity. Based on our understanding of Rogers's declaration cited above, such radical humanism should be first understood within a very specific framework, cultural tradition, and system of thought. Incontestably, Soyinka's humanism is connected to his work of intellectual activism and cultural criticism. Soyinka is a trans-continental public intellectual whose commitment to the good and welfare of humanity is aligned with the Western humanist tradition. We concur that his public intellectualism is also shaped by the life and politics of continental Africa, and the plight of the African people.

In his acceptance speech, he cautious humanists to come up with a stronger rejoinder to dismantle the arrogance of imperialism and cross-cultural terrorism committed in the name of religion: "We need to deploy a new language whose message is: the world is not your jurisdiction."

Soyinka appeals to the imperative of language as an instrumentalization to wage war against religious terrorists, and to silence religious purists—such as the Boko Haram and ISIS gangs. A complementary characteristic of Soyinka's humanism is his approval of the just war theory—which excludes him from being called a pacifist; as he declares in the closing words of his speech: "Each time some wound to religious sensibilities is used to unleash terror on innocent communities, the obvious response should be: invade and inundate that space with the very material that is alleged to have given offence." Evidently, Soyinka sees "destructive weapons" as a means to foreclose the deep wounds of religion, and to fight religious terror.

> With greater details, he expounds on the call to arm to avenge the blood of the victims: An aerial bombardment with weapons of the mind—invades that space through whatever medium of transmission is feasible. If textual—pages, chapters, illustrations, word clusters floating in space, descending on church steeples, minarets, schools, farms, factories, prisons, markets and barracks, floating down on the pompous, hypocritical chambers where self-designated theologians order the arrest, torture, imprisonment, decapitations and hangings of those alleged to be enemies of an unseen deity . . . Prove even deeper the wounds of insecurity already gouged in the self-esteem of gloating, arrogant, seemingly crazed abductors—and their allies everywhere—who dance their mockery of the world on video . . . The world should wake up to the fact that the menace is borderless, aggressive, and unconscionable.[10]

In the paragraph above, it is indecisive whether Soyinka is calling upon humanist groups to collaborate together in order that they might inflict punishment on religious fanatics or has he conferred the sentence to the hands of the state? ("The world should wake up to the fact that the menace is borderless, aggressive, and unconscionable.") Given the excellent track record of Soyinka as a fierce human rights advocate and freedom fighter, it would be absurd and unreasonable that he would confer the judgment of religious extremists in the hands of individuals. As could be inferred, Soyinka endorses the just war theory which places him in the Augustinian tradition.

Soyinka submits that there exists a wide gap between religion and humanism. The creed of humanism is not compatible with the ideology of religious extremism. Both articulate competing systems and conflicting visions of the world, history, and humanity. Soyinka sees religion as a threat to the evolution of humanism in the world, and the ideals of humanism: "Perhaps Humanists should pause from time to time and ask themselves a simple, straightforward, even neighborly question: what do religionists really want? Not what they worship—that is beyond rational comprehension for many but—what do they really seek." Soyinka advances the idea that religion is predominantly responsible for the world's catastrophes: "If society appears to be foundering, and along lines that clearly indicate religious factors—the world being in no shortage of current exemplars." He expresses the same thought provocatively: "The conflict between Humanists and Religionists has always been between the torch of enlightenment and the chains of enslavement." As a result, it is the duty of humanists to deliver religion people from religious enslavement. Here, Soyinka is possibly referring to dangerous religious ideas and beliefs that trigger suicide bombing and mass destruction. In such circumstances, humanist groups are responsible to maintain "self-preservation, to understand what the various constituent parts seek for their self-fulfillment." Soyinka warns humanists and the world at large about the supposedly-harmless mission of religious radicals:

> We are speaking here of a resolute, but proliferating minority who declare their objective as the right to intervene dictatorially in the rights, mores and undertakings of others—all in the name of their presiding deity. This claim to the privileged exercise of Control is what plagues the world in ever expanding arenas of conflict, a belief that absolute authority is invested in them by a supreme, though invisible entity, to meddle in the lives of others, not even in an advisory role, not even as provider of optional guidelines, but with an absolutism that brooks no dissent.[11]

Soyinka calls this deliberate activity in which religionists exhibit a pretense of piety and propagate a climate of fear, "religious imperialism." He argues that it is erroneous to believe that religionists in general seek "to serve God;" on the contrary, their objective is to gain power, jurisdiction, and influence, by any means necessary. Soyinka construes "the myrmidons of religious imperialism not simply as a threat to human freedom but also a challenge to tolerance and peace, "indeed the all-out assault on humanity."

We have noted in our previous analysis that Soyinka does not attribute religious discomfort to a few individuals of the religionist camp, but to all religions and religious zealots, whose ultimate objective is to proselytize others to their faith. Soyinka construes the act of proselytization or religious conversion as a transgression to humanist creed and a distraction to religious pluralism: "Fundamentally, in spite of the prominence of schisms in the intensification of religious carnage, we should avoid distraction by the claims of one set of beliefs against another." As can be observed, Soyinka's reasoning on religion is not absent of intellectual conflict and paradox. Soyinka supposes that those who use religion as a weapon to oppress people are not worthy of religious freedom. At what point should the State censor religious freedom without violating the freedom of expression? Soyinka attempts to respond to this difficult question by relating it to another equally valid matter. Soyinka's unconditional preference for religious relativism is not always evident in his writings. We shall return to this issue shortly in the conversation.

Arguably, the arrogance of faith expressed especially "when one sect promotes the supremacy of precedence, to which a purity—and authenticity—of belief is then attached, as against later 'corruption,' against which an orgy of purification is then launched." The stubbornness of religion is also entrenched on the absolute claim of truth such as the Bible or the Qur'an is God's revelatory word, and the unrelenting conviction that the Bible is the supreme source of authority to provide guidance in matters of faith and practice. Soyinka rejects this proposition on ideological grounds:

> The proposition that the original Scroll of beliefs, known sometimes as Scriptures, Was one of imperfection, the hidden conclusion of which has merely laid in wait in the wings, presumably to see how humans doom themselves in advance with the worship of false gods—until the emergence of Absolute Truth, ideally signaled by the appearance of a charismatic preacher.[12]

Soyinka's linguistic exaggeration and ideological supposition about the passion of religious zealots should be taken in consideration. The failure of these individuals is that they have no interest in interfaith and ecumenical dialogue to improve relationship between the religions: "All too often they lead directly to the gallows, to beheadings, to death under a hail of stones. In numerous parts of the world today the Scroll of Faith is indistinguishable from the Roll-call of Death."[13] Yet, Paul Copan has expressed a competing position that "institutionalized pluralism and diversity in society can have the effect of excluding and eliminating traditional religion from the conversation."[14] He adds, "Properly understood, we actually need more religion, not less. But we need the right kind of religious values, not simply anything that calls itself religious (think Jim Jones, David Koresh, and jihadists)."[15] It is evident that Copan believes that some religions are not promoting the "right values" conducive to the welfare of humanity and a democratic life in the present or future.

By stating that Christianity provided the foundation for morality and has positively influenced Western civilization and other cultures, Copan is proclaiming Christian exceptionalism and triumphalism, and ultimately, the superiority of Christianity over other religions.[16] To put it another way, unlike the religious critic Wole Soyinka, the Christian philosopher Paul Copan has no problem affirming the divine inspiration and credibility of the Bible or accept the Bible as the "infallible Word of God."

On the contrary, Soyinka has not only problematized the human disposition to total submission to the sacred text of a particular religion, he has also interrogated the hermeneutical paradigms and interpretive lens by which the preacher or the guardian of the faith interprets the text, uncovers its meaning, and communicates the message to the devotees.

> What humanity has reaped from these Scrolls of Faith, pulled down from nowhere in the firmament by those who have been considered sages, prophets, messiahs etc. is one that has manifested itself historically as inimical to human inclusiveness and social cohesion. Yet such Scrolls continue to be advertised as documents that deserve human adulation, treated with reverence even by non-believers. Not even though disputes over the interpretation of their tenets—and even history—such as their coming-in-being—have spilled over millennia, continue till today, and have never ceased to foment strife of an increasingly virulent nature.[17]

Soyinka discards the very notion of "Scriptural infallibility" and the "historical reliability" of sacred texts, as maintained by adherents of Judaism, Christianity, Islam, and thinkers on the theological right. Such belief is seen as a threat to the doctrine of radical humanism and religious relativism: "It is such scrolls, treasured as infallibility made flesh, that make the creed of humanism not only a necessary counter but a human imperative." For the Nigerian religious critic, the theological doctrines of conservative religions are at stake with the values and principles of humanism. The practice of religious intolerance and bigotry makes the co-existence of religion in society an uncomfortable issue, and "dooms the very enthronement of civilized forms of interaction, while opening thoroughfares of blood and destruction." African philosopher Kwasi Wiredu has articulated a critical position parallel to that of Soyinka about the nature of truth, dogmatism, and scriptural authority:

> The concept of absolute truth appears to have a tendency to facilitate dogmatism and fanaticism which lead, in religion and politics, to authoritarianism and, more generally, to oppression. Indeed, if human beings were always consistent, the doctrine of absolute truth should lead to total skepticism rather than to dogmatism . . . It is a fact, nevertheless, that in matters of truth and falsity, drastic persecution is hardly conceivable without pretensions to absolute truth on the part of the persecutions . . . Dogmatism, obversely, consists not just in expressing one's opinions with positive conviction but in the unwillingness or refusal to offer evidence for them or to consider objections with a view to revising them.[18]

When truth is not conceived as opinion, as Wiredu maintains, the possibility for religious antagonism and interfaith discontent is inexorable. For example, Bernard Lewis in *Islam and the West* reflects the ambivalent nature of these three faiths: "Traditional Christianity and Islam differed from Judaism and agreed with each other in that both claimed to possess not only universal but exclusive truths. Each claimed to be the sole custodian of God's final revelation to mankind. Neither admitted salvation outside its own creed."[19] Consequently, religion in general is perceived as a transnational and cross-cultural conundrum. Soyinka places nonprogressive faiths among the global problems that defer human solidarity and progress. In the lecture, he advises his humanist audience: "The subject of Religion is one that must be brought openly to the table with other national and global concerns—poverty, social welfare, corruption, shelter, soil erosion, hunger, disease, environment degradation and all other societal mandates."

Soyinka's clarion call for the absolute abandonment of religious certainties, and religious exclusivism has its foundation in his deliberate embrace of inclusive cultural relativism and general cultural diversity. It will perhaps be constructive for our conversation to explore his thought on the sensitive issue of cultural relativism in the Geneva Lectures Series he delivered in December 10, 2008 in Geneva.

Soyinka's goal in the lecture was to help his spectators avoid the "trap" of cultural relativism, as the lecture is rightly entitled "The Avoidable Trap of Cultural Relativism." Soyinka is neither a blind cultural relativist nor a fierce defender of unconditional cultural diversity. He understands the potential pitfalls and shattering consequences of inclusive cultural relativism and general cultural diversity on human life, societies, and civilizations.

First, Soyinka provides a sophisticated definition of cultural diversity as to the willingness to open up to foreign cultures and acknowledge "the richness of man's creative existence and palpable manifestations of his inner sensibilities, his aesthetic impulses and sometimes even his spiritual intuitions." Secondly, cultural relativism entails "expressions of solidarity among, cultures, an affirmation of the right to differing expressions of cultural production, social mores and values." At this junction, both proposed definitions seem to sustain Soyinka's program of generous tolerance and challenge the arrogance of faith and religious imperialism. It promotes the politics of responsibility and relationality.

The implementation of these concrete ideas into practical cultural life and the human experience is very promising and can hypothetically lead to more tolerance and respect for people, their culture and religion. Cultural diversity and cultural relativism seem to hold the promise to bar rituals of exclusion which precondition and divide the human race and cultures hierarchically, racially, and in an opposing binary category: the good and the bad, the civilized and the barbarian, Christian and pagan, western and non-western, etc.

Hitherto, Soyinka forewarns his Genevan audience about the strictures and liabilities of cultures and societies that deliberately proclaim cultural relativism and an all-inclusive environment without restriction:

> Human society is shaped as much by climatic conditions—whose diversity also cannot be denied—as by history—including the origins of such societies, and the experience of external encounters. Cultural relativism claims to imbue us with a respect for these differences. In practice however, it asks us accept such barbarisms as "honor killing" as justified by tradition, or dictatorship, even of the most brutal kind, as sanctified by a people's antecedent or ongoing experience, largely under duress, conveniently labelled political culture. It endorses the rights to discriminate between sexes, between races, and to accept the stratification of citizens on grounds of religious beliefs, color of skin or gender.

Following this commentary, he moves forward to discuss two momentous events in modern history: the apartheid culture of South Africa and the triumph of Hitlerism in Western Europe in the first half of the twentieth century. His projected and desired goal is to alert about the perils in accepting an all-encompassing worldview. Cultural relativism is certainly a trap when it is used to profit those in power and influence.

> A trap of course, a cunning device meant to lure the unwary into the counterfeit face of mutual tolerance of, and respect between cultures, that is, breed an attitude that legitimizes any form of conduct, as long as it can be attributed to cultural usage. It is a cynical design disguised as a mechanism for the promotion of the virtues of Diversity, deployed mostly by men in a position of power and their apologists. We encountered it, for instance, among the justifications for the creation of Bantustans.
>
> Humanity is of course diverse. So, logically, are the products of his hand and mind, and sensibilities—culture above all else. Is it however possible to conceive of the relativity of one member of the human species to another? That would be to endorse the Nazi doctrine of racial selectivity and thus, of disposable humanity. The innate properties of each human unit, what collectivity defines us as social beings in contrast to the rest of the anima world, cannot be relative—not if we accept that all sentient beings, despite their diversity, meet at a common destination known as humanity, and that all its members are indeed born with such innate properties.

In the next phase of the lecture, Soyinka emphasizes the significance of social responsibility and mutual accountability; he also comments on how to vitiate the negative effects of cultural relativism especially when it infringes on individual and collective freedom and defers the common good:

> What circumstances of birth, upbringing, opportunities and environment make of each is a different matter, but cannot be considered fundamental to the worth and validity of each individual, and thus to his or her entitlements from, and responsibility to the rest of society, in the pursuit of self-development and social relationships. The issue comes down, as always, to a contest between power and freedom, or human volition, and the desire of the former to encroach upon, and dominate the latter. Thus is laid that red herring, cultural relativism, evoked to make a hierarchical distinction between spaces of power and spaces of freedom. Part of our social responsibility is to come to the defense of the latter. Freedom, above all else, is guaranteed by a plurality of choices . . .

Soyinka prioritizes human rights and freedom over cultural relativism: "We have to address those societies and states which either fail to recognize this, or elect to evoke entitlement of cultural relativism in order to undermine or dismiss the universalist entitlement of human rights." To move the conversation forward, Soyinka turns our attention to the principles of generous tolerance of the Yoruba religious system; he recommends that we extract wisdom from the Ifa divination system in order that we might be able to ameliorate the human condition in the world and enhance communication between the religions:

> Our repositories of exclusive spiritual truths can learn from this ancient, unassuming faith of our forebears. Ifa is tolerance. Ifa takes issue with any religion or faith that denies tolerance a place in its worship. Ifa embodies the principle of the constant, spiritual quest, one to which the notion of apostasy is unthinkable . . . Tolerance is perhaps the most relevant, the most sorely in demand in our global dilemma . . . Tolerance, in its own right, is at the heart of Ifa, a virtue worth cultivating as a foundational principle of humanistic faith—the catechism of the secular deities, a spirit of accommodativeness . . . [20]

Adama & Naomi Doubmia in *The Way of the Elders* provides a balancing commentary to Soyinka's declaration:

> Beliefs of many faiths have swept through our land. The African spiritual approach allows for the integration of different religious practices with its own. Many among us maintain our traditional beliefs and feel comfortable accommodating ideas from other faiths. Any tradition where Spirit is at the heart of its practice finds its home in Africa. [21]

The philosophy of generous tolerance is intertwined with the religious ideology and culture of the Yoruba people, and African humanism. Soyinka redirects our attention to the nature of truth in Yoruba moral vision:

> The Yoruba understanding of the nature of truth is indeed echoed by the Verdict texts from yet another ancient world, the Indian, which declares:

"Wise is the one who recognizes that Truth is One and one only, but wiser still the one who accepts that Truth is called by many names, and approached from myriad routes.

Its equivalent will be encountered in the well-known pronouncement of an African sage, known as the Sage of Bandiagara, of Mali:

There exists your truth, there is my truth and there—the Truth."[22]

To complement his stated thesis, he takes us to the world of the Yoruba gods themselves who have modelled a divine attitude of "spiritual accommodativeness":

> The accommodative spirit of the Yoruba gods remains the eternal bequest to a world that is riven by the spirit of intolerance, of xenophobia and suspicion. This spirit of accommodation, this habit of ecumenical embrace is not limited to the domestic front or to internal social regulations . . . To understand the instructional value of this in relation to other religions, one has only to recollect that, for some religions, even today, the interpretation of their scriptures in relation to human inventiveness is toward foreclosure, so that modern innovations in the technological and cultural fields are simply never permitted . . . Authority for the exclusionist approach to new phenomena is always extracted from or attributed to their scriptures—the Bible, the Koran, or the Torah.[23]

> Ifa's tenets are governed by a frank acknowledgement of the fact that the definition of truth is a goal that is constantly being sought by humanity, that existence itself is a passage to Ultimate Truth, and that claimants to possession of the definitiveness of knowledge are, in fact the greatest obstacles to the attainment of truth. Acceptance of the elastic nature of knowledge remains Ifa's abiding virtue, a lesson that is implanted in the Yoruba mind by the infinitely expansible of the gods themselves. Is it any surprise that in Orisa religion, the concept of infallibility in doctrinal matters, or Revelation as the last word, does not exist? If emphasizes for us the perpetual elasticity of knowledge.[24]

To recapitulate his argument, Soyinka urges us to interrogate claims of "absolutes—not merely for the culture under the scrutiny but for the scrutinizing size which, even without so declaring, has already positioned itself on legitimate critical grounds, often presumed higher." In his autobiography *Ibadan: The Penkelemes Years—A Memoir 1946–65*, he introduces various expressions to signify the uncertainty and improbability of (absolute) truth such as "half-truth," "doctored truth," "selective truth," "annotated truth."[25] Further, he encourages us to defy networks of power that sustain ostentatious cultural relativists and publicists of cultural diversity who are less concerned to foresee their snares on human society:

> The very phenomenon of power and its exertion over others is very much part of the discourse, and it assists in clarifying one's position to a large extent,

power being a craving that sometimes manifests itself in a need to impose conformity, to dictate, or to intrude in matters of choice that stress the singularity of the human entity.[26]

Soyinka consents with many critical thinkers that cultural relativism "is not the talismanic mantra for the resolution of the human predicament—indeed, it is only the beginning of a complex, ethically rigorous exercise, not its terminus."[27] As Sam Harris has concluded in his insightful analysis about the demon of relativism, "Moral relativism, when used as a rational for tolerance of diversity, is self-contradictory."[28] Interestingly, moral relativism and cultural relativism are compatible with the principles of humanism.

Soyinka articulates his strong conviction and devotion to the tenets and objectives of radical humanism:

1. "Society is built on the practical, unavoidable principle of co-existence."
2. Radical humanism is committed to "human inclusiveness and social cohesion."
3. "Humanism requires a new tactical language, and what language requires a drastic shift in emphasis."
4. "We must take on the duty of telling the enemy openly: it is spiritual fulfillment that you seek but—Power. Control. Power in its crudest form."
5. "Humanism requires developing a distinct philosophy of transformative aggression."
6. "There comes a time when our humanity accepts that there must be an end to an attitude that is best captured in that Yoruba expression: *F'itiju k'arun*. Literally that means—contracting a disease through politeness. Translated yet again, this time into the fashionable language of social morbidity that mistakes sophistry for sophistication, it reads simply: *Political Correctness*."
7. Radical humanism is committed to "The elevation of humanity, the enhancement of its productive potential, or the harmonization of its relationship with power and authority."[29]

In the closing words in the Geneva Lectures Series, Wole Soyinka calls for immediate action to end the savagery and barbarity of religion:

> The ultimate purpose remains: to dent the sanctimonious self-righteousness of those who question our right to volition and human dignity. Collectively, we must eradicate the enclaves of religious atavism with human alternatives, new vistas of the world, new insights into history, new propositions of human relationships—of gender, race, beliefs, classes and identifies. Above all, however—ACT! That imperative is upon us, will it or not. Act in a resolute

manner that demonstrates that humanity is not so supine that it will absorb obscene affronts to its defining right of dignified existence.

Elsewhere in *Climate of Fear*, Soyinka's rhetorical appeal is hasty and aggressive: We have a duty therefore to use very opportunity to disseminate efforts that counteract such moments of divisiveness and retrogression . . . Still lacking, however, is a manifest global commitment, especially a sustained and dynamic reciprocity from rival cultures and religions . . . The globe needs to be saturated, almost on a daily basis, with such encounters . . . There is nothing in the least delicate about the slaughter of innocents. We all subscribe to the lofty notions contained in the Universal Declaration of Human rights but, for some reason, become suddenly coy and selective when it comes to defending what is obviously the most elementary of these rights, which is *the right to life*.[30]

Moreover, Soyinka establishes a close connection between democratic freedom and generous tolerance, which sustains human dignity and sustainable development:

We consider also a dispensation that enables all humanity to breathe freely, to associate freely, to think freely, and to believe or not to believe without a threat to their existence and without discrimination in their social rights. Implicit in that freedom of association is, difficult as it may be to accept, the right of collective dissociation.[31]

CONCLUSION

To bring our analysis to an end, we should reiterate that the Yoruba religious framework provides the resources to heal the world, cultivate friendship, and to live a life marked by human solidarity, comradery, interdependence, and relationality:

We aim to cultivate a spiritual ingenuity recognizing synchronicity, coincidence, and the messages all around us. We strive to know ourselves and our special roles in the universe . . . We surrender to the ebb and flow of life, and cultivate an ability to both yield to and direct the life force. We strive to maintain harmony with the rhythms of the universe . . . As we are all connected, it is essential to realize that our spiritual progression is both an individual and a communal effort. We work to create healing and regenerative energy. We look within, and we also, importantly, look outside of ourselves, taking responsibility for the effects of our actions on everything around us. We explore our relations with family, friends, community, earth, and spirits.[32]

The gist of Soyinka's message of radical theistic humanism and generous tolerance—enclosed within the Yoruba religious world and ethical values—is "the belief in eventual tolerance and mutual generosity of sufficient strength to transcend historic memory."[33] Secondly, Soyinka gives primacy to the moral vision of African traditional religions and spirituality because of their susceptibility to accommodate other faiths and competing ideologies resulting in a spirit of tolerance, liberalism, charity, and religious pluralism.[34] We must remind ourselves that "religion provides society is not just high-mindedness, but also a concern with the quality of life—a goal more ennobling than the simple accretion of power and possessions."[35] Based on Soyinka's reasoning, African spirituality and African theistic humanism in particular animate optimism, grace, and openness toward a more promising future for all people and for all faith.

> Sources of conflict between nations and among peoples exist in the struggle for economic or natural resources as much as in the tendency toward the tyrannical temper of ideas, be these secular or theological. For the latter, the problem does not really lie with Christianity or with Islam, Judaism, or Hinduism, etc., but with the irredentist strain that appears to have afflicted these world religions, unlike the order of the Orisa. We need to remove the veil over these invisible religions and ask again: why is it that the Orisa has never, in all these centuries, spawned an irredentist strain. Orisa separates the regulation of community from spirit communion even while maintaining a mythological structure that weaves together both the living community and the unseen world. But that world of the spirit does not assume any competitive posture whatsoever over the pragmatic claims of the real world . . . Volition, not submission, sums it up . . . If the humanity were not, the deities would not be. Humanity, not deity, is the begetter of metaphysics.

In the final chapter of the book, we have argued unlike Western humanism, Soyinka's radical humanism is theistic and deeply informed by Yoruba cosmology and the principle of inclusive tolerance of the Orisa. Soyinka projected that only through our embrace of the values and wisdom of the Orisa would we be able to eradicate religious violence, terrorism, and imperialism in the twenty-first century global culture. Soyinka's radical theistic humanism, which promotes unqualified tolerance and challenges claims of absolutes and certainties of the religious brand, is an adequate alternative to foster human solidarity and build optimistic and democratic societies in this present world. If violence is the engine of religious banditry and fundamentalism, open-mindedness is the fuel of radical theistic humanism. Soyinka views African spirituality and African humanism as a liberative presence in the modern world against the arrogance of faith and religious imperialism.

NOTES

1. Ngũgĩ, wa Thiong'o, *Decolonizing the Mind*, 87.
2. Williams, "Religious Humanism," in Anthony Pinn (ed), *By These Hands*, 33–4.
3. Gyekye, *Tradition and Modernity*, 158–9.
4. Gyekye, *An Essay on African Philosophical Thought*, 143.
5. Gordon, *An Introduction to Africana Philosophy*, 186.
6. Gyekye, *An Essay on African Philosophical Thought*, 143–4.

7. Soyinka, *Climate of Fear*, 98.
8. Ibid.
9. Ibid., 99–104.
10. The International Humanist and Ethical Union (IHEU). 12 August, 2014. Interested readers can read the entire speech online: http://iheu.org/wole-soyinkas-international-humanist-award-acceptance-speech-full-text/
11. Ibid.
12. Ibid.
13. Soyinka, *Of Africa*, 155–6.
14. Copan, *Is God a Moral Monster?* 199.
15. Ibid.
16. Ibid.
17. The International Humanist and Ethical Union (IHEU). 12 August, 2014. http://iheu.org/wole-soyinkas-international-humanist-award-acceptance-speech-full-text/
18. Wiredu, *Philosophy and an African Culture,* 122–3.
19. Lewis, *Islam and the West*, 175.
20. Soyinka, *Of Africa*, 164–5.
21. Adama & Naomi Doubmia, *The Way of the Elders*, 158.
22. Soyinka, *Of Africa*, 151–2.
23. Ibid., 152–3.
24. Ibid., 155–6.
25. Soyinka, *Ibadan: The Penkelemes Years*, x.
26. Soyinka, *Of Africa*, 177.
27. Ibid.
28. Harris, *The End of Faith*, 179.
29. Soyinka, *The Open Sore of a Continent*, 115.
30. Soyinka, *Climate of Fear*, 85–6.
31. Soyinka, *The Open Sore of a Continent*, 142.
32. Adama & Naomi Doubmia, *The Way of the Elders*, 156–7.
33. Soyinka, *Myth, Literature, and the African World*, 77.
34. Ibid., 79.
35. Juergensmeyer, *Terror in the Mind of God*, 246.

Appendix

Wole Soyinka: Chronology

1934

- Born Oluwole Akinwande Soyinka on 13 July 13, in Abeokuta, near Ibadan in western Nigeria. Son of Samuel Ayodele and Grace Eniola Soyinka

1946–1950

- Attended the prestigious Government College in Ibadan.

1952–1954

- Studied Literature and languages (French and Greek) at University College, Ibadan.

1954

- Fulfilled preparatory university studies at Government College in Ibadan.
- Moved to England to complete studies in drama at Leeds.
- Published "Keffi's Birthday Treat" (Short Story)

1954–1957

- Attended the University of Leeds (Northern London)
- Graduated with B.A. in English Honors in 1957.

1957

- Olaokun (son) born in November.
- Wrote "Madame Etienne's Establishment" (Short Story), and "A Tale of Two Cities" (Short Story)

1958

- Married British writer, Barbara Dixon.

1958–1959

- Served as dramaturgist at the Royal Court Theater in London 1958–1959.

1960

- Nigeria became an independent state.
- *A Dance of the Forests* was first performed as part of the Nigerian Independence Celebrations, in October 1960.
- Wrote "Egbe's Sworn Enemy" (Short Story), and "Toward a True Theatre" (Essay)
- Received a Rockefeller research grant to study African drama, and Nigerian traditions and culture.
- Returned to Nigeria.
- Established the theatre group called "The 1960 Masks."

1962

- Served as Lecturer in English at the University of Life.
- Resigned from the post in protest of the undemocratic public policies of the Western Nigerian regional government.

1963

- Married Nigerian librarian, Olaide Idowu
- Moremi (son) is born in February.

1964

- Became very active in Nigerian Politics.
- Founded the Drama Association of Nigeria.
- Created the Orisun Theatre Company.

1965

- Became Senior Lecturer at the University of Lagos.
- Briefly arrested for political activism.
- Published *The Interpreters* (Novel)

1966

- Nigerian Civil War begins

1967–1969

- Published a controversial article demanding cease-fire during the Nigerian Civil War.
- Accused of conspiring with the Biafra rebels.
- Held in the Kaduna prison in northern Nigeria for 22 months as a political prisoner.

1967

- Published *Idanre and Other Poems* (Collection) (Poetry)
- Awarded the John Writing Drama Award

1968

- Awarded the Jock Campbell-New Statesman Literary Award for his first novel, *The Interpreters*.

1969

- Released from Prison in 1969.
- Became Head of the Department of Theatre Arts at the University of Ibadan.
- Published Poems from Prison (collection) (Poetry), and "The Writer in a Modern African State" (Essay)

1970

- Forced into exile.

1971

- Resigned from his University Post.
- Settled in Accra, Ghana.
- Published *A Shuttle in the Crypt* (collection) (Poetry)
- Wrote *Before the Blackout* (Play)

1972

- Published *The Man Died: The Prison Notes of Wole Soyinka* (Autobiography). (The memoir was banned in Nigeria in 1984.)
- Awarded an honorary PhD from University of Leeds.

1973

- Served as Visiting Professor at the University of Sheffield and Fellow of Churchill College, Cambridge.
- The National Theatre in London premiered the play, *The Bacchae of Euripides*.
- Wrote *A Dance of the Forests: The Swamp Dwellers; The Strong Breed: The Road; The Bacchae of Euripides (Collected Plays I)* (Play)
- Published *Season of Anomy* (Novel)

1974

- Cofounded the Union of Writers of the African Peoples and is elected Secretary General.
- Wrote *The Lion and the Jewel; Kongi's Harvest; The Trials of Brother Jero; Jero's Metamorphosis; Madmen and Specialists. (Collected Plays II)*, *Before the Blackout and Camwood on the Leaves* (Play), and *Camwood on the Leaves* (Play)

1975

- Returned to Nigeria.
- Appointed Professor of Comparative Literature at the University of Ife.
- Wrote "Death and the King's Horseman" (Play)
- Published "Neo-Tarzanism: The Poetics of Pseudo-Tradition" (Play), and *Poems of Black Africa* (Poetry)

1976

- The French translation of the play, *The Dance of The Forests*, was performed in Dakar, Senegal.
- Wrote "Ogun Abibiman (collection)" (Poetry)
- Published *Myth, Literature and the African World* (Essay)

1977

- Served as Administrator of the International Festival of African and Negro Arts and Culture (FESTAC) in Lagos, Nigeria.

1978

- Published "Language as Boundary" (Essay)

1981

- Became Visiting Professor at Yale University.
- Published Aké: The Years of Childhood (Autobiography)
- Wrote "Opera Wonyosi" (Play)

1982

- Released the film *Blues for the Prodigal.*
- Published "Cross Currents: The 'New African' After Cultural Encounters" (Essay)

1983

- His memoir, *Aké: The Years of Childhood* won the Anisfield-Wolf Book Award.
- Wrote "Requiem for a Futurologist" (Play)
- Published "Shakespeare and the Living Dramatist" (Essay)

1984

- Wrote "Sixty-Six," and "A Play of Giants" (Play)

1985

- Delivered the, "Climates of Art" for the Herbert Read Memorial Lecture at the Institute of Contemporary Art (London).
- Named President of UNESCO's International Theatre Institute.

1986

- Soyinka became the first African to win the Nobel Prize in Literature.
- Received the Agip Prize for Literature.
- Conferred with The Nigerian National honour of Commander of the Federal Republic (CFR)
- Became Fellow, Society for the Humanities at Cornell University.
- Published "The External Encoutner: Ambivalence in African Arts and Literature" (Essay)

1988

- Published *Art, Dialogue, and Courage: Essays on Literature and Culture* (Essay)
- Wrote "Mandela's Earth and Other Poems" (Poem)

1989

- Married AdeFolake Doherty
- Published *`Isarà, A Voyage Around "Essay"* (Autobiography)

1990

- Became the leader of movement against the military dictatorship in Nigeria.
- Received the UK Royal Society of Literature's Benson Medal.
- Published *The Blackman and the Veil: A Century on; And, Beyond the Berlin Wall* (Essay)

1991

- Broadcast on BBC Radio 4 *A Scourge of Hyacinths*.

1992

- Wrote "From Zia with Love" (Play)

1993

- Received honorary doctorate from Harvard University.

1994

- Fled Nigeria
- The United Nations Educational, Scientific and Cultural Organization (UNESCO) named Wole Soyinka a Goodwill Ambassador for the promotion of African culture, human rights and freedom of expression.
- The Nigerian government of General Sani Abacha confiscated his passport.
- Published *Ibadan: The Penkelemes Years, A Memoir: 1946–1965* (Autobiography)

1995

- Protested against the cancellation by the military regime of the federal elections won by Moshood Abiola.
- Launches an international campaign against the Nigerian dictatorship.

1996

- Forced into exile from Nigeria.
- Appointed as Robert W. Woodruff Professor of the Arts of Emory University.
- Published *The Open Sore of a Continent: A Personal Narrative of the Nigerian Crisis*. The book is named one of the 25 best books by The Village Voice.
- Wrote "The Beatification of Area Boy" (Play)

1997

- Charged (in March) with treason and sentenced to death in *absentia* by the Nigerian military regime of Sani Abacha.
- Published *Early Poems* (Poetry)

1998

- Returns to Nigeria.

1999

- Published *The Burden of Memory, The Muse of Forgiveness* (Essay)

2000

- Published *The Credo of Being and Nothingness* (Essay)

2001

- The play *King Baabu* premiered in Lagos.
- *Conversations with Wole Soyinka edited* by Biodun Jeyifo (Essay)
- Wrote "King Baabu" (Play)

2004

- Wrote *Climate of Fear: The Quest for Dignity in a Dehumanized World* (Essay)

2005

- Conferred with the chieftaincy title of Akinlatun of Egbaland

2006

- Published *You Must Set Forth at Dawn: A Memoir* (Autobiography)

2009

- Received the Academy of Achievement Golden Plate Award in the United States.

2011

- Wrote Alapata Apata (Play)

2012

- Won Obafemi Awolowo Leadership Award on December 19

2013

- Won the Anisfield-Wolf Book Award (for lifetime achievement)

2014

- Won the Internationalist Humanist Award from the International Humanist and Ethical Union and the British Humanist Association

Bibliography

Access Bank hosts Professor Wole Soyinka in Ghana." Ghana Business News. 3 July 2015.https://www.ghanabusinessnews.com/2015/07/03/access-bank-hosts-professor-wole-soyinka-in-ghana/
Andrew, Lang. *The Making of Religion*. Charleston: BiblioBazaar, 2009.
Armstrong, Karen. *Holy War: The Crusades and their Impact on Today's World*. New York: Anchor Books, 2001.
Banham, Martin, Hill, and George Woodyard (eds). *The Cambridge Guide to African and Caribbean Theatre*. Cambridge: Cambridge University Press, 2005.
Berstein, Richard J. *Radical Evil: A Philosophical Interrogation*. Maldon: Polity Press, 2002.
Bruce, Steve. *Politics & Religion*. Cambridge: Polity, 2008.
Carnois, Bernard. *The Coherence of Kant's Doctrine of Freedom*. Chicago: University of Chicago Press, 1987.
Copan, Paul. *Is God a Moral Monster? Making Sense of the Old Testament God*. Grand Rapids: Baker Books, 2011.
Dawkins, Richard. *The God Delusion*. Boston: Houghton Mifflin Company, 2006.
Dennett, Daniel C. *Breaking the Spell: Religion as a Natural Phenomenon*. New York. Penguin Books, 2006.
Doubmia, Adama, and Naomi Doubia. *The Way of the Elders: West African Spirituality & Tradition*. Saint Paul: Llewellyn Publications, 2004.
de Vries, Hent. *Religion and Violence: Philosophical Perspectives from Kant to Derrida*. Baltimore: The John Hopkins University Press, 2002.
Durkheim, Emile. *The Elementary Forms of the Religious Life*. Translated by Karen E. Fields New York: Free Press, 1995.
Gibbs, James (ed). *Critical Perspectives on Wole Soyinka*.Washington: Three Continents Press, 1980.
Gikandi, Simon, ed. *Death and the King's Horseman: Authoritative Text Backgrounds and Contents Criticism*. New York: W. W. Norton & Company, 2003.
Gordon, Lewis. *An Introduction to Africana Philosophy*. Cambridge: Cambridge University Press, 2008.
Gyekye, Kwame. *An Essay on African Philosophical Thought: The Akan ConceptualScheme*. Philadelphia, 1987.
———. *Tradition and Modernity: Philosophical Reflections on the African Experience*. New York: Oxford University Press, 1997.
Harris, *The Moral Landscape: How Science Can Determine Human Values*. New York: ree Press, 2010.

———. *The End of Faith: Religion, Terror, and the Future of Reason.* New York: W. W. Norton & Company, 2005.
Hicks, John. *An Interpretation of Religion: Human Responses to the Transcendent.* New Haven: Yale University Press, 1989.
———. *God Has Many Names.* Philadelphia: The Westminster Press, 1982.
———. "Religious Realism and Non-Realism: Defining the Issue." In "Religious Realism and Non-Realism: Defining the Issue." In *Is God Real?* Joseph Runzo (ed). New York: St. Martin's Press, 1993. 3–16.
Hitchens, Christopher. *God Is Not Great: How Religion Poisons Everything.* New York: Twelve, 2007.
Idowu, E. Bolaji. *African Traditional Religion: A Definition.* Maryknoll: Orbis Books, 1975.
———. *Olódùmarè: God in Yoruba Belief.* Ikeja: Longman, Nigeria, 1982.
———. "God." In *Biblical Revelation and African Beliefs.* Kwesi Dickson & Paul Ellingworth (eds).Maryknoll: Orbis Books, 1969.17–29.
Juergensmeyer, Mark. *Terror in the Mind of God: The Global Rise of Religious Violence.* Berkeley: University of California Press, 2000.
Lewis, Bernard. *Islam and the West.* New York: Oxford University Press, 1993.
Maxwell, David, and Ingrid Lawrie (eds). *Christianity and the African Imagination: Essays in Honour of Adrian Hastings.* Boston: Brill Academic Publishers, 2013.
Mbiti, John S. *Introduction to African Religion.* London: Heinemann, 1987.
———. *African Religions & Philosophy.* Portsmouth: Heinemann, 1990.
Mudimbe, V. Y. *Tales of Faith: Religion as Political Performance in Central Africa.* London: The Athlone Press, 1997.
Netland, Harold. *Encountering Religious Pluralism*: *The Challenge to Christian Faith & Mission.* Downers Grove: InterVarsity Press 2001.
———. *Dissonant Voices: Religious Pluralism and the Question of Truth.* Grand Rapids: William B. Eerdmans Publishing Company, 1991.
Ngũgĩ, wa Thiong'o. *Decolonizing the Mind: The Politics of Language in African Literature.* Portsmouth: Heinemann, 1997.
Olupona, Jacob K. *African Religions: A Very Short Introduction.* New York: Oxford University Press, 2014.
Robin, Corey. *Fear: The History of a Political Idea.* New York: Oxford University Press, 2004.
Sanneh, Lamin. *West African Christianity. The Religious Impact.* Maryknoll: Orbis Books, 1998.
Schwartz, Regina M. *The Curse of Cain: The Violent Legacy of Monotheism.* Chicago: University Of Chicago Press, 1997.
Senghor, Leopold Sedar. "Negritude: A Humanism in the Twentieth Century." In Tejumola Olaniyan and Ato Quayson (eds). *African Literature: An Anthology of Criticism and Theory.* Malden: Blackwell Publishing, 2007.195–202,
Soyinka, Wole. *Ake: The Years of Childhood.* New York: Vintage International Edition, 1981.
———. *Isara: A Voyage Around "Essay."* New York: Vintage International Edition, 1989.
———. *Ibadan: The Penkelemes Years: A Memoir 1946–65.* London: Minerva, 1994.
———. *You Must Set Forth at Dawn*: A Memoir. New York: Random House, 2006.
———. *Art, Dialogue, and Outrage: Essays on Literature and Culture.* New York: Pantheon Books, 1988.
———. *Climate of Fear: The Quest for Dignity in a Dehumanized World.* New York: Random House, 2004.
———.*Of Africa.* New Haven: Yale University Press, 2012.
———. *The Open Sore of a Continent: A Personal Narrative of the Nigerian Crisis.* New York: Oxford University Press, 1994.
———. *The Burden of Memory, The Muse of Forgiveness.* New York: Oxford University Press, 1999.
———. *Myth, Literature, and the African World.* New York: Cambridge University Press, 1976.
———. *Death and the King's Horseman: Authoritative Text Backgrounds and Contents Criticism.* New York: W. W. Norton & Company, 2003.

———. "Theatre in African Traditional Cultures: Survival Patters." In Richard Olaniyan (ed). *African History and Culture*. Ibadan: Longman, 1982. 237–49.
———. "Psychopaths of Faith vs. The Muse of Irreverence." *New Perspectives Quarterly* 23: 2 (2006): 13–16.
———. "Neo-Tarzanism: The Poetics of Pseudo-Tradition." *Transition* 48 (1975): 38–44.
———. "Wole Soyinka's International Humanist Award Acceptance Speech." The International Humanist and Ethical Union (IHEU). 12 August, 2014. http://iheu.org/wole-soyinkas-international-humanist-award-acceptance-speech-full-text/
———. "Wole Soyinka: 'If religion was taken away I'd be happy.'" *The Telegraph*. 12 Oct 2012. Accessed July 6, 2012. http://www.telegraph.co.uk/culture/hay-festival/9600954/Wole-Soyinka-If-religion-was-taken-away-Id-be-happy.html.
Tillich, Paul. *The Essential Tillich*. Chicago: University Of Chicago Press, 1999.
———. *Systematic Theology. Volume 1: Reason and Revelation Being and God*. Chicago: University Of Chicago Press, 1973.
Townes, Emilie M. *Womanist Ethics and the Cultural Production of Evil*. New York: Palgrave MacMillan, 2006.
Williams, Jones R. "Religious Humanism: Its Problems and Prospects in Black Religion and Culture." In Anthony B. Pinn (ed). *By These Hands: A Documentary History of African American Humanism*. New York: New York University Press, 2001. 25–54.
Wiredu, Kwasi. *Philosophy and an African Culture*. Cambridge: Cambridge University Press, 1980.
———. *Cultural Universals and Particulars: An African Perspective*. Bloomington: Indiana University Press, 1996.
Zacharias, Ravi. *Can Man Live Without God?* La Porte: Thomas Nelson Publisher, 2004.

Index

Abrahamic religions, 62, 63
Africa, 20; African deities, 57; African humanism, 53–59, 71; African indigenous spirituality, 63–64, 67; African traditional religion, 53–62, 83–84; sacrifice of Africa, 63–68
African indigenous faiths, 14
African cosmology, 15
Allah, 18
Anglicanism 2, 2
atheism, 49
authoritarianism, 3

Bible, the, 22, 76; Word of God, 76
Boko Haram, 6, 18, 47, 73–74
Buddhism, 28, 33

Christianity, 4, 14, 18, 34, 62, 65, 77; Christian concepts, 28; Christian exceptionalism, 76; Christian monotheism, 58; Christian teachings, 22; Christian triumphalism, 76
Christopher Hitchens, 42–43
conversion, 67
cultural relativism, 78–79, 80

Daniel Dennett, 49
domination, 42, 46

E. Bolaji Idowu, 53, 58–59
evil, 43

faith, 18, 75; ancestral faith, 54–55; arrogance of faith, 76; end of faith, 19; psychopaths of faith, 47; scroll of faith, 76; shipwreck of faith, 21; theistic faiths, 56; world's great faiths, 29
freedom, 40, 45, 83
freedom fighter, 74, 79

Ghana, 4
God, 16, 23, 24, 26, 55, 75; Christian God, 16, 20–22; concepts of God, 55; concept of God in Africa, 55–63; God's attributes, 55, 62

Hitlerism, 79
Humanism, 24, 33, 54, 63, 71–73; creed of humanism, 75; radical humanism, 9, 36, 82–83; religious humanism, 72
human condition, 32–33
human dignity, 6, 8, 9, 73
human nature, 40
human solidarity, 71

Islam, 6, 18, 48, 62, 67, 77; Islamic Jihadism, 18

Jews, 62
John Mbiti, 53

Kwama Gyekye, 72
Kwasi Wiredu, 77

Lannin Sanneh, 66
Leopold Sedar Senghor, 53–54, 60

missionaries, 65
monotheism, 58, 61
Muslims, 4, 17, 48, 62, 66

Negritude, 7; nothingness, 40–41
Ngugu wa Thiong'o, 71
Nigeria, 2, 4, 14; Nigerian Christians, 14; Nigerian Muslims, 14; Postcolonial Nigeria, 14

Ogun, 5
Orisha, 18, 56, 57, 60

Paul Copan, 46, 76
Paul Tillich, 56
peace, 45
polytheism, 59
philosophy, 35
postcolonialism, 65
power, 46

Qur'an, 76

Ravi Zacharias, 56
race, 44
radical atheism, 42
radical skepticism, 13
radical theistic humanism, 54
religion, 7, 13, 45, 49, 55; African traditional religion, 50, 53, 57; non-theistic religions, 35; religious alienation, 30; religion and evil, 43; religious fanaticism, 32; religion and fear, 30–31, 45; philosophy of religion, 25–28; religious ideologies, 19, 26, 28, 42, 43; religious inclusivism, 13, 34, 47; religion and race, 44; religion and society, 29–31; religious skepticism, 36; religious tolerance, 14, 47, 48; religious violence, 13, 39, 40, 43–44, 60; religious zealotry, 33–34, 40, 45, 48, 75; revelatory religions, 29; Yoruba religious tradition, 13
Richard Dawkins, 43

Sam Harris, 82
Soyinka, 1, 14; & Boko Haram, 14, 18, 73–74; education, 3, 16; religious ideas, 16, 39; renouncement of Christianity, 16, 24; shipwreck of faith, 21, 23
secularism, 30–31
secular African deities, 58
solidarity, 1

terrorism, 74
tolerance, 49; generous tolerance, 9, 80
totalitarianism, 3
truth, 59, 77, 80
Theater, 17; West African theater, 17

V. Y. Mudimbe, 65
Violence, 1, 13, 54; religious violence, 13

war, 74
Western Christianity, 67

Yoruba, 15, 53, 59; Yorubaland, 15, 56; Yoruba gods, 81; Yoruba religious cosmology, 49, 59, 60; Yoruba worldview, 15

About the Author

Dr. Celucien L. Joseph is currently an Assistant Professor of English at Indian River State College. He received his Doctor of Philosophy from the University of Texas at Dallas, where he studied Literary Studies and Intellectual History. Professor Joseph also holds an M.A. in French language and literature from the University of Louisville. In addition, he holds degrees in theological and religious studies. He serves in the editorial board and Chair of The Journal of Pan African Studies Regional Advisory Board; he also the curator of "Haiti: Then and Now." He edited JPAS special issue on Wole Soyinka entitled "Rethinking Wole Soyinka: 80 Years of Protracted Engagement" (2015). Dr. Joseph is interested in the intersections of literature, history, race, religion, theology, and history of ideas.

    Professor Joseph is the author of several books including *Race, Religion, and the Haitian Revolution: Essays on Faith, Freedom, and Decolonization* (2012), *From Toussaint to Price-Mars: Rhetoric, Race, and Religion in Haitian Thought* (2013), *Haitian Modernity and Liberative Interruptions: Discourse on Race, Religion, and Freedom* (2013), *God Loves Haiti* (2015). He has also contributed several encyclopedia entries and scholarly articles in various journals. He is the lead editor of *Vodou in Haitian Memory: The Idea and Representation of Vodou in Haitian Imagination* (Lexington Books, 2016), and *Vodou in the Haitian Experience: A Black Atlantic Perspective* (Lexington Books, 2016). He is currently working on a volume on Jean-Bertrand Aristide, former President of Haiti and Catholic-Priest Liberation Theology entitled *Aristide: A Theological and Political Introduction* (under contract with Fortress Press).

www.ingramcontent.com/pod-product-compliance
Lightning Source LLC
Chambersburg PA
CBHW021146230426
43667CB00005B/269